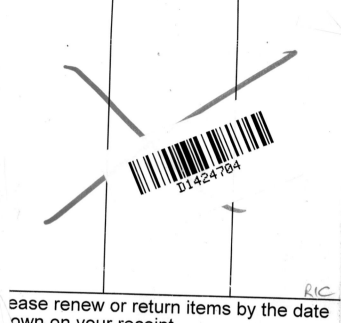

RIC

Hertfordshire

TOP 10 ATTRACTIONS

Essaouira With its port, markets and beautiful medina, this makes a delightful excursion (page 75)

Koutoubia Mosque Visible from almost everywhere in the city, the 12th-century minaret is one of Marrakech's oldest and most distinct monuments (page 30)

The souks Colourful, noisy, exotic, exhausting, tempting crowded, chaotic – a full blo to all the senses (page 32)

Ourika Valley When the buzz of the medina becomes too much, head for this quiet and beautiful valley (page 69)

Madrassa Ben Youssef The beautifully decorated 16th-century Qur'anic school is open to non-Muslims (page 40)

Badi Palace It took an army of craftsmen more than 25 years to finish Ahmed el-Mansour's splendid palace (page 49)

Guéliz Colonial architecture, shopping and some of Morocco's most exciting restaurants and nightlife (page 57)

Majorelle Gardens The contrasting electric blue walls make the green of French painter Jacques Majorelle's – and later Yves Saint Laurent's – exotic garden look all the greener (page 65)

Saadian Tombs The 66 royal tombs are notable for their lavish Andalusian-style decoration (page 46)

Jemaa el-Fna At dusk this becomes one of the world's liveliest squares, with food stalls and a host of performers (page 28)

A PERFECT DAY

9.00am **Breakfast**

Bask in the calm of a Marrakech morning with hot Moroccan bread, fresh orange juice and coffee from the terrace of your *riad* or on the sunny roof of Kechmara (see page 111) in the new town.

11.30am **Souks**

Dive into Marrakech's famed souks – a colourful, exotic labyrinth crammed with everything from sequined *babouches* to hand-woven carpets. Punctuate the shopping at Café des Epices (see page 107) in the bustling Spice Square.

1.00pm **Lazy lunch**

Stop for a bite to eat on a rooftop terrace overlooking the medina at Terraces des Epices or Café Arabe (see page 107), or spend a lazy hour or two by the pool at Beldi Country Club just outside town.

3.00pm **New Town art**

Explore the eclectic art galleries of Guéliz at Galerie 127, David Bloch Gallery, Matisse Gallery, Galerie Tindouf, Galerie Ré and Lawrence Arnott Gallery.

10.00am **Imperial grandeur**

Head to the golden tombs of the Saadian kings before the crowds arrive, then wander over to the enchanting Bahia Palace, where ornate salons and leafy courtyards are illuminated in the morning sun.

IN MARRAKECH

6.30pm   **Sunset at Jemaa el-Fna**

There is only one place to be in Marrakech at sunset and that's in the heart and soul of the city – Jemaa el-Fna, where acrobats, storytellers, magicians and fragrant food stalls fill the square, transforming it into one of the greatest spectacles in the world. Wander through the square, or have a drink at Le Marrakchi (see page 108) which has great views over it.

10.30pm   **Cocktails**

Marrakech comes alive late at night and Le Comptoir (see page 111) is the place to be, where belly dancers circulate among the in-crowd. Have a cocktail here then head to Pacha, Silver or Teatro if you fancy dancing 'til dawn.

4.30pm   **Hammams**

Back in the medina, have a glass of mint tea at literary café Dar Cherifa (see page 37), then treat yourself to a steamy traditional Moroccan *hammam* with full body *ghassoul* scrub and a rejuvenating massage with essential oils at Les Bains de Marrakech.

8.00pm   **Arabian Nights**

Dine in one of Marrakech's celebrated *riad* palace restaurants. At Dar Yacout, Dar Moha or Le Pavillion (see page 108), sit under a canopy of stars in a courtyard lit by a thousand lanterns.

CONTENTS

INTRODUCTION

M arrakech – 'the Red City' and capital of the Great South – is arguably the most exotic, mysterious and enchanting place this close to Europe. Its thousand-year history is about as rich as it is possible to be with an eclectic cast of characters, from sultans and slave-traders to colonialists, rock stars and artistic icons.

In the 1960s and '70s, Marrakech lured hippies, playboys, rich expats and the fashion elite. Today, Marrakech is experiencing its latest renaissance. With spectacular *riads* in the ancient medina that are straight out of *A Thousand and One Nights*; atmospheric imperial palaces and mysterious ancient ruins; kaleidoscopically colourful souks; a fabulous array of restaurants, bars, cafés and art galleries in the Ville Nouvelle (New Town); tranquil villa retreats; some of the best boutique five-star hotels in the world and a wealth of adventures to be had virtually on its doorstep, this desert city at the crossroad of cultures has reinvented itself yet again as a hip, romantic and adventurous getaway.

Location, Location, Location

Marrakech owes its existence, its character and its new-found success to its location. Sitting at the foot of the High Atlas Mountains and at the southern end of the lush Moroccan plains, it came into being as a market town where mountain Berbers and Arabs from the plains came to trade with the trans-Saharan caravan merchants.

The city's souks were packed with ivory, senna, ebony and slaves from beyond the Sahara, rugs and jewellery from the mountains and glass, spun cottons, teapots and weapons from

The medina walls

the north. The new tourist developments play to one of the city's strengths: its climate. Although the high summers can be blisteringly hot, winters are usually mild and often sunny, spring and autumn invariably blissful. Add to that the exoticism of the souks and the lure of the nearby snow-capped mountains, visible from medina rooftops, and it is easy to see why so many people are enchanted by Marrakech. The city is home to well over one million people, but unofficially the number is thought to be closer to two million, one third of whom are members of several Berber tribes originally from the Rif and Atlas mountains.

Yet as well as a playground for foreign visitors, Marrakech remains a vibrant Moroccan city and one that punches above its weight. It may no longer be the capital, as it once was – Rabat on the Atlantic coast has that honour – but for a long time it has been the country's most famous city.

Rahba Kedima, or Spice Square

Eighteenth- and early 19th-century Europeans called the city and the country by the same name, just as they did Algiers and Algeria, Tunis and Tunisia: in many ways, Marrakech remains synonymous with Morocco.

The Heart of the Matter

Courtyard of a restored *riad*

The city is divided into several distinct districts, the best-known being the medina – the old city inside the walls, which dates from 1070. Until little more than a century ago the miles of rust-red, mudbrick walls enclosed the entire city. Behind the series of gates, some of them seemingly straight out of fairy tales, lies a town sub-divided by interior walls and gates into distinct districts: one for the royal palaces, one – the Mellah – for the Jews, one for the souks and so on.

The medina remains the main attraction. It is a place where narrow, winding alleys unite communities around the pillars of the mosque, the school, the bakery, the *hammam* and the clusters of courtyard houses known as *riads*. The medina has few large hotels (with the sole exception of the world-famous Mamounia, built just inside the Bab Jdid, the New Gate), but what it does have are more than 800 *riads* converted and available to rent, by the room or in their entirety, by visitors.

In spite of the influx of visitors, the medina has retained much of the character and interest that led to it being inscribed on Unesco's World Heritage list in 1985. In particular, it has preserved its unique centrepiece: the Jemaa el-Fna, a triangular space beside the souks. By day, 'La Place', as it is known locally, serves nothing more exciting than juice from

Souss oranges and a few herbal medicines. At night, however, it is completely transformed. Part of the space is devoted to food stalls, where foreigners rub shoulders with local people to sample couscous, fish, sheep's head, snails and a long list of other local delicacies. The rest is taken up by entertainers, among them sufi musicians, magicians, snake charmers, storytellers and many others who fancy their chances of attracting a ring of spectators around them.

New Town Marrakech

The French were the first to build seriously outside the walls, beginning soon after 1912 when Morocco was colonised. Their Ville Nouvelle, which takes its name, Guéliz, from a small hill nearby, was laid out as a suburb of broad leafy avenues and large detached houses. It remains distinct from the medina, although it is no longer as sedate as it once was (the exception being the garden area known as Hivernage, which still has some fabulous early 20th-century villas). Other parts of Guéliz, particularly around the central artery of Avenue Mohammed V, are super-swanky and are the place to find the city's most elegant boutiques, bars and restaurants. Here, too, is one of Marrakech's most popular sights, the house and garden created in the 1920s

Majorelle Garden

by French painter Jacques Majorelle, who brilliantly combined local greens with a shade of cobalt paint now known as Majorelle blue. Twenty years ago you would have been laughed at for wanting to live in the Palmeraie, but the area of palm groves beyond the French-built new town has now become home to some of the city's wealthiest residents and some of its most

Garden city

From its foundation, Marrakech was a city of gardens. A growing population has meant that there are now few public green spaces inside the medina, but many *riads* have fig, palm or orange trees in their courtyards. Marrakech beyond the walls is still very green in places such as Hivernage, the Palmeraie and the Cyber Parc, Agdal and Majorelle Gardens.

beautiful hotels. A road snakes through the palm groves off the main Marrakech–Fez road, and the Palmeraie circuit, although no longer as calm as it once was, still runs through an area of great beauty.

The Marrakech Brand

It had been coming for a few years, but when the Moroccan government paved the way for budget flights from Europe and international-brand clubs opened their doors, it was clear that Marrakech had arrived as a key destination on the global party circuit. Following on from Ibiza and St Tropez, it has reinvented itself as the playground for wealthy Europeans, where billionaires and the slightly less well-off come to have fun.

King Mohammed VI has played a key role in recreating Marrakech, making it the centrepiece of an ambitious plan to increase tourism revenue. This has involved more than opening the skies to numerous airlines and promoting nightclubs and new hotels. Marrakech now also has beautifully restored public buildings, a lively arts and cultural scene and a growing market for upscale products, many of which find their way into Western luxury stores. The Marrakech International Film Festival grows in stature each year and several fledgling literary, art and music festivals have begun to attract attention. All this provides entertainment for visitors who want even more than stunning landscapes, extraordinary architecture, a wonderful climate and a welcome that goes far beyond a glass of sweet mint tea.

Out of Town

Many visitors who choose to stay in the medina find themselves looking for distraction beyond the confines of the city's red walls. Happily, it is easy to get out of town and there are plenty of entertainments nearby, from large, luxurious swimming pools to country club-style retreats tucked away in rose gardens. All this, and the glory of the High Atlas mountains just a short drive away, makes Marrakech the perfect place for a holiday packed with contrasts.

High Atlas

A BRIEF HISTORY

Marrakech began as an outpost of a Saharan kingdom, became the capital of an empire that stretched up to the Pyrenees, and was ruled over by some of the most colourful and extraordinary people in the long history of Morocco. Its value lay in its location, on the crossroads of trans-Saharan trade routes linking mountain and plain, desert and coast.

The city's history is not short of incident, nor of romance, bloodshed and brilliance. It seems to seep through every wall of every alley and hang over every tea-punctuated conversation.

Morocco's Dynasties

Marrakech owes its unique character to its history. Although it sits on the northern side of the great barrier of the Atlas Mountains, it was created by people from the south. The Almoravids, a confederation of Berber tribes from the Sahara, were inspired and united by Ibn Yassin, a holy man from the Souss Valley (southeast of today's Agadir), who preached a pure form of Islam. With

Berber village in the Atlas mountains

him they declared a *jihad* (holy war) against the influence of the Andalucian Moors, who allowed alcohol to be drunk and men to take more than four wives. Their zeal carried them to victory beyond the Atlas, where, around 1070, they founded Marrakech.

Marrakech was originally the Almoravids' northernmost

settlement. But the Almoravid leader, Youssef ben Tachfine, had ambitions in the north. In 1075 he conquered the central city of Fez and within five years, he had control over most of what is now Morocco, effectively creating the first Moroccan state. Before the 11th century, the country we know as Morocco was divided into many different tribal territories, Arab city-states and contested trade routes.

Youssef ben Tachfine didn't stop there. Ten years later he crossed the Straits to Spain, where the Catholics were claiming victories over the Andalucian Muslim princes. He was successful there too, and his son Ali ben Youssef, who succeeded him in 1107, inherited an empire that stretched from West Africa to the Pyrenees, from the Atlantic to Algeria. The Almoravids brought with them the technology necessary for surviving in the desert. In Marrakech, they built *khettara*, underground irrigation channels, to supply their new city with water from the Atlas Mountains.

Towers such as the minaret of the Koutoubia Mosque owe their origin to the great Almohad sultan Yacoub el-Mansour

The Almohad Princes
Although the Almoravids over-extended themselves, it is more likely that the dynasty fell because their reformist zeal began to wane. In their place rose another reformist Berber dynasty,

from the Atlas Mountains, inspired by a preacher by the name of Ibn Toumert. Ibn Toumert's targets were obvious: the Almoravids allowed their women to ride horses and had been increasingly corrupted by Andalucian ideas. The movement gathered momentum after the preacher's death thanks to the military genius of his successors, particularly the third Almohad sultan, Yacoub el-Mansour.

Master builder

Ali ben Youssef was one of the great early builders: in what is now Algeria he created the mosque of Tlemcen, and in Fez he built the central Karaouine Mosque. In his capital, Marrakech, he built the mosque and madrassa that bears his name. The carving in all the monuments was done by masters brought over from Andalucia.

Sultan Yacoub earned his title 'el-Mansour', the Victorious, for his exploits in Spain, where he defeated the Christians in 1195. He pushed east as far as Tripoli as well, and for the first time united the Maghreb under a single ruler, based in Marrakech.

He built across the empire, most notably constructing the Koutoubia in Marrakech, and beginning work on the Tour Hassan in Rabat – both of which served as models for the Giralda in Seville. The Bab Agnaou (the ornate gate into the Kasbah) is another reminder of the Almohads' austerely beautiful taste in architecture.

The dynasty was doomed soon after Yacoub's death. His successor, Mohammed en-Nasr, moved against the Christians in Spain, hoping to push them beyond the Pyrenees. His defeat at Las Navas de Tolosa in 1212 was the start of a rapid decline: in less than half a century, the Almohads lost most of their Spanish territories, including Seville, and were then edged out of Algeria, Fez and eventually Morocco. With them went Marrakech's prominence: the Merenid dynasty that succeeded

Madrassa Ben Youssef

them, and which ruled Morocco for three centuries, made Fez their capital.

The Saadians

For more than 500 years, Morocco had been ruled by Berber dynasties which had come from the south. But in the 16th century, as a result of increasing Portuguese control along the Atlantic coast, an Arab dynasty, the Saadians, rose to prominence in the Souss, building a base in Taroudant in the Souss Valley.

The defining moment for the dynasty came in 1578, when the youthful King Sebastian I of Portugal invaded Morocco, in order to support the claim of the deposed Saadian ruler Abu Abdallah Mohammed II against his uncle, Abd Al-Malik Saadi, and thereby reclaim Portugal's coastal bases. The ensuing 'Battle of the Three Kings' at Ksar el-Kebir (near Larache in northern Morocco) ended in the death of all three protagonists, and the decisive defeat of Portuguese forces.

The man who benefited from this was Ahmed el-Mansour, who became sultan in 1578. He created an army strong enough to march across the Sahara and take control of Timbuktu, the key to the trade in sub-Saharan gold and slaves.

The Golden One

They called Ahmed el-Mansour 'Eddahbi', the Golden, and with good reason, for he restored the country and Marrakech's wealth and standing. Under Sultan Ahmed, the city once more became a glittering centre of patronage. He built a magnificent palace, Badi, 'the Incomparable', and its name was no exaggeration: no building in the region came close to it in grandeur. Elsewhere in the city, Ahmed's monuments included the rebuilt Madrassa Ben Youssef and the Saadian Tombs, the compound where he and his dynasty were buried in tombs that match the magnificence of the finest Andalucian work (see page 46).

The Cruel Sultan

Moulay Ismail (1672–1727) was one of the more bloodthirsty characters of Moroccan history. With an army of 150,000 African mercenaries he drove the Portuguese out of their Atlantic strongholds, the Ottomans back to the current frontier with Algeria and the English out of Tangier. For Marrakech and the other imperial city, Fez, his reign was a disaster. Wanting to avoid the glorification of earlier dynasties, Moulay Ismail destroyed all traces of them and set about creating what he hoped would be the greatest of all Moroccan cities, Meknes, 60km (38 miles) from Fez. His palace complex, intended to rival Versailles (and today a Unesco World Heritage Site), was built using materials looted from Saadian palaces. It took Ismail's workers 12 years to strip Marrakech's Badi palace of all its treasures.

But like many despots before and since, Ahmed failed to establish a clear successor and on his death in 1603, his descendants fought over the throne, weakening central rule so much that within just a few decades the empire had crumbled.

The Alaouites

As before in Morocco's history, change came like a breath of hot wind from the south. While the Saadians fought among themselves, the Alaouites, a tribe who originated from the oases of the Tafilalt and claimed descent from the Prophet Mohammed, began to unite southern tribes around their base in Rissani, on the edge of the Sahara. It wasn't until 1669, more than half a century after Ahmed's death, that the Alaouite Sultan Moulay Rachid moved on Marrakech. Rachid held power for just three years before being killed in a palace coup. In contrast, his successor the tyrannical Moulay Ismail ruled for 54 years and laid the foundations of the dynasty that continues to rule Morocco today.

Ismail's heirs were less successful, as his numerous sons (he is said to have fathered more than 1,000 children) disputed the throne for 30 years. Once again power fractured and the kingdom went into a long, slow decline throughout much of the 18th century. Marrakech went with it. Without stability, the trade routes no longer flourished.

But a succession of sultans exploited foreign interest and for more than a century played the British off against their rivals, the French and

Glaoui's palaces

T'hami el-Glaoui grew immensely wealthy by controlling trade, both legal and illicit, in the High Atlas south of Marrakech. With some of the proceeds, he built palaces, among them a magnificent Kasbah in the mountains at Telouet and the Dar el-Bacha in Marrakech.

Spanish, for a stake in the nation's commerce.

French Protectorate

The Moroccan sultans held out against European pressure for more than a century. But in 1912, the ruling sultan Moulay Hafid signed an accord, the Treaty of Fez, that effectively handed over sovereignty to France and made the country a French colony with its capital in Rabat.

Marrakech had a central role to play in the story of French colonisation. French forces struggled to take control of the tribes in the south, where the landscape, climate and the nature of the tribal communities were impossible to subdue. With the outbreak of World War I, the French did not have the manpower to fight their way through the region. Instead, the French governor General Hubert Lyautey made a deal with the most powerful family in the High Atlas, the Glaoui, who collaborated with the French and imposed their rule.

Depiction of early 19th-century Marrakech

Armed by the French and left to their own devices, the Glaoui brothers, Madani and T'hami, earned a reputation as 'Lords of the High Atlas'. Their tribal base was in Telouet, but they ruled the mountains and the trade routes south of Marrakech and in 1912 T'hami el-Glaoui took the title of Pasha of Marrakech.

Until the period of French control, Marrakech was mostly confined within its walls, but the colonisers planned European districts – the Ville Nouvelle (New Town) – outside the walls, where the garden suburbs of Guéliz and Hivernage were laid out.

Independence

There was resistance to French rule from the moment it began, but the Moroccan independence movement became viable only after the French defeat by Germany in World War II. However, it wasn't until the early 1950s, when the movement had such popular support that the French felt the need to exile the sultan (later king) Mohammed V to Madagascar, that the outcome became inevitable.

In 1955, Mohammed V returned and in March the following year, choosing to concentrate their efforts on holding

Mausoleum of Mohammed V in Rabat

Algeria, the French (and soon afterwards the Spanish) recognised Moroccan independence. T'hami el-Glaoui, the Pasha of Marrakech, who had hoped to exploit the sultan's departure by expanding his influence, died two months before independence but after switching his support to Mohammed

V, who was crowned king and oversaw the creation of the modern state.

Hassan II and National Identity

Mohammed V's eldest son, King Hassan II, who took the throne in 1961, dominated the country for the remainder of the 20th century. Although ostensibly a constitutional monarch, Hassan ruled the country with an iron and rigidly conservative fist. In 1975, he furthered Morocco's claim to Western Sahara and encouraged 350,000 Moroccans to occupy the region in what has become known as the *Marche Verte* (Green March). This is an occupation that continues today and continues to be disputed. The latter decades of Hassan II's rule – darkened by the imprisonment, torture and disappearances of opponents and dissidents – came to be known as the 'Years of Lead'. He survived two assassination attempts in the 1970s and died in 1999.

A New Era

When Mohammed Ben Al-Hassan was crowned Mohammed VI in July 1999, Morocco entered into a new era. The new king was intent on forging pioneering reforms. Early on in his reign, he overhauled the *Mudawana* or family code, based on Islamic law, which would fundamentally change the lives of Moroccan women and, even more extraordinarily, established the Equity and Reconciliation Commission, which investigated abuses from his father's reign. At the same time, Mohammed VI saw the need to establish closer ties with the west as well as increase foreign investment in Morocco, particularly noticeable in the tourist mecca of Marrakech, which has seen a boom in the building of tourist hotels and resorts. Mohammed VI remains a popular figure but his reign has not been above criticism – or without problems.

The shadow of Islamic fundamentalism reared its head in suicide bombings in Casablanca in 2003 and in Marrakech in 2011; the issue of Western Sahara remains contentious and in spite of strong UN attempts to broker an agreement between both sides, the deadlock continues. In 2011 the Arab world was rocked by revolution and change and though Mohammed VI remains in power, his rule has been tested by protests, which to some extent he has heeded – amending the constitution and devolving more of his powers to the prime minister. How far he will go and how long he will escape the kind of regime change affecting other countries in the region remains to be seen.

King Mohammed VI

Historical Landmarks

1062 The Almoravids, a Berber fundamentalist dynasty founded by Youssef ben Tachfine, establish Marra Kouch (Marrakech) as their new capital.

1126–7 The first city walls are built.

1147 The Almohads destroy most of the Almoravid monuments, replacing them with their own, including the impressive Koutoubia Mosque.

1184 The city's golden age under Yacoub el-Mansour sees a flourishing of arts and science.

1269 The city goes into decline when the ruling Merenids chose Fez as their capital.

1551 The Saadians re-establish Marrakech as the capital of an empire that stretches from the Niger river to the Mediterranean.

1668 The Alaouite dynasty, from whom the current King Mohammed VI is a descendant, comes to power.

1672 The Alaouite ruler Moulay Ismail moves the capital to Meknes, and the city once again falls into decline for several centuries.

1912 Treaty of Fez makes Morocco a French Protectorate. The French start building a new city (Ville Nouvelle) outside the medina walls. The French appoint T'hami el-Glaoui as Pasha of Marrakech and ruler of the south. He and his brother Madani were known as 'Lords of the Atlas' and were notoriously cruel.

1956 Morocco becomes independent under Mohammed V. El-Glaoui dies two months before independence.

1980s Massive rural exodus towards the cities makes Marrakech Morocco's second largest city.

1999 Mohammed VI becomes king on the death of his father, Hassan II.

2001 First International Film Festival in Marrakech.

2009 Fatima Zahar Mansouri becomes Marrakech's first female mayor.

2010–2011 Peaceful protests are held across Morocco, demanding constitutional reform. The majority of Moroccans remain supportive of the king.

2011 Nail bomb detonated in Jemaa el-Fna in Marrakech. 17 people killed. No one claims responsibility.

WHERE TO GO

Most visitors to Marrakech go in search of the exotic and year-round sunshine but the city also has a variety of sights that reveal its character and bear witness to its rich history. Most of these sights are in the medina (old city), an area that can be explored easily on foot. This will allow you to take in some shopping in the souks. The historic monuments are often places of peace and tranquillity, sheltered from the buzz of the city. At first the medina may seem a confusing warren of alleyways and markets, but soon landmarks begin to stand out and the basic ground plan reveals itself, especially as there are only a few main axes through the souks.

The Ville Nouvelle (New Town), also called Guéliz, has some remarkable gardens and is the place to find Western-style shopping, art galleries and more varied restaurants and entertainment than in the medina. The Palmeraie, just outside town, is a pleasant place for cycling and also has some of Marrakech's most exclusive hotels, villas and golf courses. For a glimpse of the countryside around Marrakech, head to the beautiful Ourika Valley or to the peaks of the Atlas Mountains.

JEMAA EL-FNA AND AROUND

The medina of Marrakech is surrounded by well-preserved **city walls** made of *pisé* (clay dried in the sun). These alter their shade with the changing light of the day, from ochre and deep orange to pink and purple. Almoravid Sultan Ali ben Youssef built these 16km (10-mile) -long walls in 1126 to protect the city against the threat of Almohad Berbers

Former Qur'anic school Madrassa Ben Youssef

Activity hots up as night falls on Jemaa el-Fna

from Tin-Mal up in the High Atlas. The walls are nearly 10m (33ft) high and have 200 towers and 20 gates. It was once a great outing to take a horse-drawn carriage (*calèche*) around the medina, but the busy road beside it now makes this less enjoyable. The gates and walls are better explored from inside the medina.

Jemaa el-Fna

The fabulous square of **Jemaa el-Fna** ❶ is the heart and soul of the old city and one of the liveliest places in Morocco, if not in the world. It is the obvious starting point for a tour. The area around it is dotted with budget hotels and small restaurants serving all kinds of delicious food. Overlooking the square is the surviving minaret of the Koutoubia Mosque (see page 30). Next door, is the more contemporary Cyber Parc, with efficient public internet booths at its heart. The old and the new cohabit happily in Marrakech.

The origin of the name of this most famous of Moroccan squares is lost, its meaning disputed. One source translates Jemaa el-Fna as 'Assembly of the Dead', a reference perhaps to the fact that it was used as a place of public executions. But rather than a place of death, 'La Place', as locals refer to it, is very much alive and kicking for most of the day and night, so much so that over the centuries it has become a showcase for popular and traditional culture. Activity starts early, around 9am, when orange juice vendors set up their stalls. Soon after appear colourful water sellers, along with snake charmers, dancing monkeys and potion sellers. In the late afternoon the arena in front of the juice stalls becomes busy with storytellers, reciting old Arab tales, with Gnaoua musicians singing their trance-like songs and acrobats building human pyramids. After the sun goes down the atmosphere becomes even more frenzied with more performers, larger crowds, a cacophony of noises and music, transvestite belly dancers, passionate storytellers and comic acts, all caught up in the swirling smoke and scents of hundreds of stalls selling excellent street food, from kebabs to a soup of snails.

Street food

Boubbouches Snail soup
Brochettes Grilled meat on skewers
Calamars Fried squid
Couscous Steamed semolina with meat and vegetable stew
Harira Chickpea soup
Merguez Spicy sausages
Tagine de poulet Chicken stew
Tête d'agneau Sheep's head
Kefta Grilled meatballs

Koutoubia Mosque

In 2001, its importance was recognised when Unesco declared it an outstanding example of the world's intangible cultural heritage. It is easy to understand why, for the Jemaa el-Fna is not just part of today's Marrakech, but captures something of the past and the future, and is a fascinating arena of human interaction. Try to have at least one meal in the square, sharing a bench with locals around a stallholder grilling meat on skewers or scooping up piles of couscous. Afterwards join the impromptu circles around performers to watch a show. When it all gets too much, head for one of the rooftop terraces around the square for a bird's eye view, and an espresso or a cup of mint tea (no alcohol in these places, except the restaurant La Marrakchi). Beware of pickpockets at night.

The Koutoubia Mosque

Some 300m/yds southwest of Jemaa el-Fna is the largest tower in Marrakech, the iconic **minaret** of the **Koutoubia Mosque** ❷ (closed to non-Muslims). The elegant minaret, nearly 70m (230ft) high, rises dramatically above the city. A building rule introduced by the French decreed that no building in the medina should be higher than a palm tree, and no building in the Ville Nouvelle higher than the Koutoubia.

The Almohads destroyed the earlier Almoravid mosque and palace, the scattered remains of which can be seen just north of the mosque. Sultan Abdel Moumen started building the mosque in 1150 shortly after conquering the city, but he didn't live long enough to complete the minaret; that honour fell to his grandson, Sultan Yacoub el-Mansour (1184–99). El-Mansour also constructed the Tour Hassan in Rabat and though it was never completed, this and the Koutoubia served as inspiration for the Giralda in Seville, Spain, which was a minaret before being converted into a cathedral.

The Music of the Gnaoua

The musicians on the Jemaa el-Fna, with their castanets, shell-encrusted caps and spinning tassels, may be performing for tourists, but they follow a long tradition. The Gnaoua are descendants of black slaves who were first brought to Morocco in the 16th century when Moroccan control of Timbuktu and the trans-Saharan caravans began. They are mystical healers who, through their music, take possession of the spirits. Using a three-stringed percussive lute (guembri), large metal castanets (qraqeb) and drums (ganga), they create rituals and initiations that are a blend of black African and Arabo-Berber elements. The most important and spectacular ceremony is the Lila Derdeba (The Night of the Stomping of the Feet), an all-night ceremony in which the music and dancing lead to a trance that enables participants to get closer to their mulk, a powerful spirit that possesses them.

Nowadays, they are called upon to perform their trance music for births, weddings and tourist shows. Every year in June the immensely popular Gnaoua Festival of World Music (www.festival-gnaoua.co.net) takes place in Essaouira. A group of young musicians, together with Gnaoua masters, have recorded an entire lila (night) of music on the CD Marrakech Undermoon: the Black Album (www.kamarstudios.com).

Mosque of booksellers

Koutoub is the Arabic for book, and *koutoubiyyin* the word for booksellers. Books, booksellers, printers, binders and scribes once occupied the maze of alleys and shops around the original mosque. Appropriately, Sultan Abdel Moumen's offering to celebrate the opening of the new mosque in 1154 was a very early copy of the Qur'an.

The Koutoubia's minaret follows the typical Almohad proprotions of 1:5 (the height being five times the width).

From the Koutoubia gardens, you can walk around the outside of the minaret. Each facade is decorated with a different pattern, and the ornamentation becomes increasingly rich and fine towards the top, ending in the only surviving strip of the original turquoise faience work. The four balls at the pinnacle of the minaret were made of pure gold and the story goes that the fourth (traditionally, there are usually only three) was a gift from Yacoub el-Mansour's wife, who sought forgiveness for breaking the Ramadan fast. The gardens are open to the public – a great place to hear the *adhan* or call to prayer.

SOUKS

Getting lost in the warren of the **souks ❸** of Marrakech is one of the city's most memorable experiences. Marrakchis have traded from the city's earliest beginnings: gold, ivory and spices came from Africa, and leather, ceramics and spices went to Europe, and it is still the city's mainstay.

The souks are a treat for the senses: the eyes feast on a dazzling display of the best of Morocco's traditional crafts; the ears ring with noise from the workshops and the constant enticement of vendors trying to sell their wares with *'Entrez, entrez, venez voire pour le plaisir des yeux...'* (Come in, come in, for the pleasure of your eyes...); the nose takes in every smell from the spice market, from the delicate scent of perfume stalls to the pungent odours of the leather tanners. The busiest times in the souks are during the morning and late afternoon, and haggling is very much part of the game when you want to buy something. It is no longer really necessary to use a guide to the souks. The labyrinthine alleys may be confusing at first but the area is relatively small, and however deep you have ventured you are never much more than a 10-minute walk from 'La Place', which is often signalled by arrows on the wall. Shopping in the souks used to be a hassle, literally, but the introduction of a 'tourist brigade' has put a stop to 'faux guides' and overly pushy shop owners and has made the whole experience more relaxed. If you would like to use a qualified guide, hire one through your hotel. Keep to the right when walking through the medina.

One Aladdin's cave after another

Souk Smarine and Rahba Kedima

The easiest way to enter the souk is via an arch on the north side of the Jemaa el-Fna, near the café Terrasses de l'Alhambra (see page 108). The covered market leads to the main artery of the souks, the **Souk Smarine**, which used to be the souk of the blacksmiths who dealt specifically with horses and donkeys. This always-busy shopping street is now mostly devoted to selling souvenirs to tourists – pottery, textiles, a few antiques emporiums - but a few shops still sell wares to local people, including celebratory circumcision outfits for boys. Au Fil d'Or at No. 10 sells good-quality traditional clothing for men and women as well as beautiful made-to-measure shirts and jackets.

After about 300m/yds, before the street forks, an alley to the right leads to the lively square of the **Rahba Kedima** ❹. Also known as Place des Epices (Spice Square), this

Cosmetics in the Spice Market

Argan oil Locally produced oil of the argan nut, known for its anti-ageing and anti-oxidant properties.

Cochineal Contained in little pottery saucers and used as lip rouge.

Dadès roses Dried roses and rose-water are used to perfume rooms and the body.

Ghassoul Body scrub used in the *hammam*.

Henna Green leaves or powder used to dye the hair, or for tattooing the hands and feet at celebrations.

Kohl Silvery antimony is ground into a powder, which gives a black out-line to the eyes and protects them from dust.

Loofah The dried sponge-like fruit of a climbing vine related to the gourd, used as a scrub in bathhouses.

Savon noir Oily black soap used in the *hammam* (Turkish bath).

Suek Walnut root or bark used as a toothbrush.

Rahba Kedima, or Spice Square

atmospheric open space, once the old corn market, is lined with shops selling spices, herbal remedies and a variety of items used in magic potions and amulets, including animal horns, skins, dried lizards, scorpions, hedgehogs and chameleons. Berber women from the Atlas sell their wares, including baskets and hats, from the middle of the square. In addition to the mountains of different spices, look out for savon beldi (local soap), a black, tar-like soap made from olives; baskets of henna leaves (plus tubes of ready-made paste); and antimony (kohl) to darken eye rims. The latter is used to protect as well as beautify: children's eyes are sometimes rimmed with kohl to ward off evil spirits, especially after birth or circumcision. On the north side of the square, past the **Café des Epices**, are two entrance ways to the **Criée Berbère** (Berber Auction). The narrow space is now mostly taken over by carpet sellers (and is *the* place to go to buy a carpet), but until 1912 this was the site of a slave

Carpets sold on the north side of Spice Square

auction held every Wednesday, Thursday and Friday before sunset. Slaves captured in Sudan or sub-Saharan Africa were brought to Marrakech with the camel caravans.

Kissaria

Just beyond the turn-off to the Rahba Kedima, the Souk Smarine artery divides in two. The alley to the right leads to the **Souk el-Kebir**, the one on the left to the **Souk des Babouches** and further on to the **Souk Kchachbia**. Between the two is the **Kissaria**, a covered market that lies at the heart of the souks. Originally this was a place where the most expensive textiles were sold, but these days it is a place to look for all sorts of fabrics and clothing, and often some less commercial souvenirs.

The Souk el-Kebir still has some woodworkers and wood turners who sell bowls, skewers and other wooden household implements. Further on is the **Souk Cherratine** where there is a traditional saddle maker, and stalls selling leather goods. Nearby, in Souk Cherifia, beneath Terrasses des Epices (see page 109), is La Galerie – a gorgeous split-level courtyard space that houses 15 quirky boutique shops which take the very best of Moroccan design – be that a lantern, a piece of jewellery or a kaftan – and work in modern twists that draw inspiration from around the world. At the end of Souk Cherratine, past the place Ben Youssef, take a right turn onto rue du Souk al Fes, which is lined with some interesting old *fondouks* (caravanserai) selling lanterns and other traditional Moroccan crafts, then onto rue Bab Debbagh, and close to the city gate the pungent smell of the nearby tanneries will hit you. It's a very smelly but interesting process to watch, even though most natural dyes have these days been replaced by chemicals. The left-hand alley off that main fork leads into Souk Kchachbia. At first this is called the Souk des Babouches, for obvious reasons: most of the stalls along here are devoted to selling *babouches*, the typical, colourful Moroccan slippers.

Further along, a cacophony of beating and hammering will lead you to the dark alley of the **Souk Haddadine** where blacksmiths forge iron into lamp stands, furniture and window grilles that now decorate so many Marrakchi interiors. Several alleys to the west of Souk Kchachbia lead to the **Souk Sebbaghine or Souk des Teinturiers** – the Dyers' Souk. Wool and scarves in a rainbow of

Take a break

Café des Epices (see page 107): sip mint tea while watching the crowds in Rahba Kedima.

Terrace des Epices (see page 109): a peaceful oasis of mint tea, fresh salads and good music in the day, and a cool hangout at night.

Dar Chérifa: a lovely literary and arts café.

Café Arabe (see page 107): a great restaurant with one of the best roof terraces in the medina.

colours are dyed and draped to dry across wires above these picturesque alleys. There are some junk shops here, and a few shops selling felt bags, carpets and elaborate silverware.

Mouassine

A small alley at the end of the Souk Sebbaghine leads to the crossroads of rue Dar el-Bacha and rue Mouassine. This is the beginning of the up-and-coming **Mouassine** ❺ area, with more up-market antique dealers at the far end of rue Dar el-Bacha, as well as several trendy boutiques along the street, on rue Sidi el-Yamani and rue el-Ksour. The palace of **Dar el-Bacha** (also known as Dar el-Glaoui) was the palace of the despotic and cruel T'hami el-Glaoui (see page 21) who ruled Marrakech and the Atlas for the French under the Protectorate. One of the city's most opulent buildings, there are plans for it to be set up as a museum to house the collection of the

Moroccan slippers (*babouches*)

late Patty Birch, an American collector of Islamic fine art and antiquities, whose beautiful *riad*, Dar Kandi, was built in 1915 for one of the Glaoui brothers. Nearby is the wonderfully atmospheric Hammam Dar el Bacha – worth a visit for those brave enough to experience a traditional Moroccan 'bath'.

Assorted metalwork

Many *fondouks* in the area have also been renovated and taken over by shops and workshops. Several European fashion designers have bought properties in this neighbourhood and this is where they shop – their favourite place is Tresor des Nomades or 'Mustafa Blaoui' (rue Bab Doukkala) an extraordinary Aladdin's Cave of treasures from around Morocco and Africa – and the fantastical, quirky art gallery-cum-design shop, Ministero del Gusto (22 Derb Azzouz; www.ministero delgusto.com).

Past rue Riad Larouss lies **Zaouia of Sidi Abdel Aziz**, the shrine of another of the Seven Saints, who died in 1508. Nearby is the ornate **Mouassine Fountain** and further left the **Mouassine Mosque** (closed to non-Muslims), built by Saadian Sultan Abdullah el-Ghalib in 1560.

As a result of these changes, Mouassine has become the place to look for something unique, if pricey.

The place Bab Fteuh offers another passage between the medina and the Jemaa el-Fna. This little square has many traditional clothing shops as well as a caravanserai where wholesalers sell Berber and other jewellery. Here, too, is the wildly expensive Akbar Delights, which sells exquisite embroidered Indian kaftans and accessories.

Detail in Madrassa Ben Youssef

THE NORTHERN MEDINA

The quieter northern part of the medina is more residential, with interesting *riads*, down-to-earth food markets, workshops and some of the best *riad* restaurants in the medina. The northern medina also includes important architectural sights.

Madrassa Ben Youssef

The green tiled roof and minaret of the **Ben Youssef Mosque**, which is not open for visits, rise above the place Ben Youssef. The Almoravid sultan Ali Ben Youssef first built a mosque here in the 12th century, but the building standing today dates mostly from the early 19th century.

Across from the mosque is the **Madrassa Ben Youssef** ❻ (daily Apr–Sept 9am–7pm, Oct–Mar 9am–6pm; charge, includes combined tickets for the Musée de Marrakech and the Koubba Barudiyin). Madrassas were residential colleges for the learning of the Qur'an, where free board and lodgings were provided to the *tolba* or students. This madrassa was founded in the 14th century by the Merenid sultan Abou Hassan, and restored in the 16th century under Saadian sultan, Moulay Abdellah, who turned it into the largest example in the country. As is usual in Islamic architecture, it has plain exterior walls, giving no hint of the staggering ornamentation inside, where every surface is covered in cedar and stucco carvings and *zellige* (mosaic tiling). Intricately executed floral and geometric motifs are repeated in mesmerising patterns, an effect intended to focus the mind on the infinite power and purpose of God.

At its height, the monastic-style cells of the Madrassa Ben Youssef could house up to 900 students. It remained in use as a religious school until 1960. From the street, a small passageway leads into a hall from where stairs go up to the students' rooms. At the end of the hall is the madrassa's main courtyard, a large open space with a central marble basin, flanked by two galleries of pillars. At the other end is the entrance to the prayer hall. The prayer hall has an octagonal domed roof supported by marble columns. The arched *mihrab*, which indicates the direction of Mecca, is beautifully decorated with elaborate stucco work. No surface is left untouched and yet the rich and elaborate stucco, cedar carving and *zellige* never overwhelm or distract from the harmony created by the use of space.

On the south side of the square is the historically important **Koubba Barudiyin** ❼ (daily Apr–Sept 9am–7pm, Oct–Mar 9am–6pm; charge) also known as the Almoravid Koubba.

Madrassa Ben Youssef

Musée de Marrakech

The two-storey domed structure covers an ablution pool that appears to be all that has survived of the Ben Youssef Mosque. It may look insignificant at first sight, but its scalloped and horseshoe arches, stepped, ziggurat-style merlons and fine arabesque patterns are all the more important and poignant in their evocation of the perfection of that period's Islamic architecture.

Musée de Marrakech

Just before the Madrassa Ben Youssef is the **Musée de Marrakech** ❽ (Marrakech Museum; www.museede marrakech.ma; daily Apr–Sept 9am–7pm, Oct–Mar 9am–6pm; charge). The palace of Mehdi M'Nebhi, defence minister and ambassador under Moulay Abdel Aziz and later Thami el Glaoui, was one of the finest built in Marrakech in the 19th century. It was bought by Omar Benjelloun, a collector of traditional Islamic arts, who restored both the palace and the nearby Madrassa Ben Youssef and Koubba Barudiyin. The museum, opened in 1997, shows temporary exhibitions of traditional and contemporary Moroccan arts.

The M'Nebhi palace is built around a splendid courtyard, with fountains, a pleasant café and a good bookshop. The interior has excellent stucco work and *zellige* tiling and some of the galleries are notable for being in the original *hammam* (bath house) and the *douira* (kitchen).

Dar Bellarj

Behind the Madrassa Ben Youssef, **Dar Bellarj** ❾ (daily 9am–1.30pm and 2.30–6pm; charge) is a former *fondouk* (caravanserai) that served as a sanctuary for storks *(bellarj)*. The Dar Bellarj Foundation has now restored the property as a cultural centre. The fine building has a peaceful courtyard and is a perfect place to escape the bustle of the souks.

Maison de la Photographie

From the Madrassa, follow the signs to the **Maison de la Photographie** ❿ (46 rue Souk al Fes; www.maisondela-photographie.ma; daily 9.30am–7pm, charge). This tiny *riad* houses the photography collection of Patrick Mana'ch. The 5,000 mesmerising photographs, dating from the 1870s to the 1950s, are beautiful testaments to a time in Morocco that has long since disappeared. Postcards, posters and books can be bought and there is a little café on the roof terrace.

North of Place Ben Youssef

The route from place Ben Youssef to the northern tip of the medina leads past the **Chroub ou Chouf Fountain**. Built in the 16th century, the fountain is one of the most beautiful examples of how important water is to the city. An inscription invites passers-by to 'chroub ou chouf – drink and look', although most people now come to this Unesco World Heritage Site to look at it, rather than drink from it. Rue Bab Taghzout, north of the fountain and relatively free of tourists, leads to Bab

Chroub ou Chouf Fountain

Taghzout, the northernmost limit of the medina until the 17th century, and beyond it the **Zaouia of Sidi bel Abbès ⓫**, the shrine of the most important of Marrakech's Seven Saints (see box). The large, mainly 18th-century mosque that houses his tomb is off limits to non-Muslims, but it is possible to take a peep at the great pyramid-like shrine and also to walk through the courtyard outside the mosque.

From there, a street leads eastwards towards **Bab el-Khemis** (Thursday Gate), a fine gate built by the Almohads. Outside it, to the north, is an interesting flea market (Souk el Khemis) where many expats and *riad* owners come in search of retro furniture.

THE SOUTHERN MEDINA

The Almohads under Sultan Yacoub el-Mansour first built their **Kasbah**, or walled citadel, in the southern part of the medina during the 12th century. The complex included palaces, barracks and the royal mosque. The Kasbah still holds

The Seven Saints

Marrakech has had the honour of being the burial place of many holy men. In 1672 Moulay Ismail declared seven of them – Sidi Cadi Ayad, Sidi es-Soheyli, Sidi Yousef bin Ali, Sidi bel Abbès, Sidi bin Sliman el-Jazouli, Sidi Abdal Aziz Tebba and Sidi el-Ghazwani – the patron saints of Marrakech. They were buried in various cemeteries around the city between the 12th and 16th centuries and a tour of their tombs became a minor pilgrimage, known as the Visit of the Seven Saints (es-Sebti) of Marrakech. This pilgrimage became so famous all over the country that Moroccans sometimes say 'I am going to the Seven Saints', meaning that they are travelling to Marrakech. The pilgrimage ends at the most important shrine, that of Sidi bel Abbès, a 12th-century holy man who was invited to the city by Yacoub el-Mansour.

the royal palace used today by King Mohammed VI when he is in town (closed to visitors). This is also where Sultan Ahmed el-Mansour built the Badi Palace (see page 49). The Saadians also chose to bury their sultans here, in the magnificent Saadian Tombs (see page 46).

Next to the Kasbah is the old Jewish quarter, the **Mellah** (see page 48), with narrow alleys, old synagogues and a colourful food market.

At the heart of the southern medina is the lively place des Ferblantiers (see page 48). From there the parallel streets rue Riad Zitoun el-Kedim and rue Riad Zitoun

Bab Agnaou

el-Jdid lead straight to the Jemaa el-Fna. The quarter is most easily visited on foot.

Bab Agnaou

The main gate into the medina was the **Bab er-Rob**, but nearby **Bab Agnaou** ⑫ gave entrance to the Kasbah. This elegant gate was ordered by the Almohad sultan Yacoub el-Mansour in 1185 and, exceptionally for Marrakech, was not built in pink *pisé* but carved in the local blue-greyish Guéliz stone. Agnaou in Berber means 'a ram without horns', referring to the fact that the gate lost its two towers, but it is more commonly believed that it means 'Gate of the Guineans', a reference to the royal guards who were brought from sub-Saharan Africa.

Immediately inside the gate is the **Mosquée de la Kasbah** (no entry for non-Muslims), which was also built by Sultan Yacoub el-Mansour and is easily recognisable by the original green tiles that decorate the minaret. This vast mosque, which has five inner courtyards, was restored by the Saadians and later by King Hassan II.

Saadian Tombs

The descendants of Prophet Mohammed, known as *shorfa*, had long been buried in the walled garden here, often in anonymous tombs, and the 16th-century Saadian dynasty chose the same place to bury their own sultans and their families. The dynasty's founder, Sultan Mohammed es-Sheikh, was buried here in 1557. Most of the exquisitely decorated *koubbas*, standing today, were built by his third son, the great conqueror Ahmed el-Mansour, for himself and his immediate family. There are 66 tombs inside and 100 outside in the gardens. Unlike the Badi Palace, which was dismantled by the later sultan Moulay Ismail and his Alaouite successors, the Saadian Tombs escaped pilfering out of superstition, though they were blocked up by Moulay Ismail. The tombs were almost forgotten until the French General Lyautey had the area surveyed from the air in 1917, and then cut a new narrow entrance through the wall. The restored **Saadian Tombs** ⓭ (daily 8.30–11.45am and 2.30–5.45pm; charge) are now one of the major attractions in town, so go early in the morning or late afternoon to avoid crowds.

The first hall to the left is the **prayer hall**. Four pillars support lofty horseshoe arches and there's a finely decorated *mihrab*. Ahmed el-Mansour connected this hall to his own tomb but didn't intend it as a burial place. Later rulers, however, were buried here, including several 18th-century Alaouite princes. An elegant arch opposite the *mihrab* leads to the central mausoleum of Ahmed el-Mansour, known as the Hall of Twelve Columns. The central tombs, flanked by 12 decorated marble columns, hold the remains of Ahmed el-Mansour, who died in 1603, with his son Zaidan to his right and grandson Mohammed esh-Sheikh II to the left. The decoration of the gilded cedar wood dome is overwhelmingly rich, with some stunning calligraphy, while the walls are covered in splendid *zellige* mosaic. Thirty-three other princes are buried here, with more in the **Hall of the Three Niches** to the right.

The **Second Koubba** in the middle of the garden was the first one to be built by Ahmed el-Mansour, and is more sober in decoration. The burial chamber, decorated with *muqarnas* (stalactites), contains the tomb of his mother, the venerated Lalla Messaouda, with a commemorative inscription. To her left is the tomb of his half-brother Sultan Abdullah el-Ghalib, and to his left the tomb of his father Mohammed esh-Sheikh. Only the torso of his father is buried here, as the Turkish mercenaries who killed him took his head to be displayed in Istanbul.

Saadian Tombs

The Mellah and Place des Ferblantiers

From the garden entrance, return to Bab Agnaou, turn right onto rue Oqba ben Nafaa and right again on avenue Houmman el-Fetouaki, which leads to the **Place des Ferblantiers** ⓮ (Tinsmiths' Square) and the Jewish quarter or Mellah.

The picturesque square, once part of a souk in the *mellah*, is a large *fondouk* now taken over by lantern makers. The square is a pleasant place for a drink and snack at one of the cafés. You could also head for the rooftop of the trendy Kosybar (see page 109) or elegant Le Tanjia restaurant (see page 109). Across the street is a covered jewellery market, the Grand Bijouterie, which was once full of Jewish goldsmiths. To the east, through the **Bab Berrima** gate, lies the **Mellah** ⓯. In 1558, nearly 100 years later than most other Moroccan cities, the Saadian sultan Abdullah el-Ghalib moved all the Jews of Marrakech into the Mellah, a secure quarter adjacent to the royal palace, entered by just two gates. The Mellah formed a city within the city, governed by a council of rabbis, which was led by a Jewish *Qaid* (leader). The Mellah had its own souk, gardens and cemetery.

The **Mellah Market** is one of the oldest food markets in Marrakech and was historically a lifeline for the Jewish quarter, which was

Place des Ferblantiers

effectively a ghetto. This is a colourful place to explore – crammed with butchers, flowers, fruit, vegetables, cosmetics and spices. The Jews were very influential traders and bankers under the Saadians and often made a living as middle-men between Muslim and Christian merchants. Before World War II, more than

Star of David tiles in the Mellah

16,000 Jews lived in the high buildings in this quarter, but after 1948 and the foundation of Israel many of them moved either there or to more cosmopolitan Casablanca. Today, fewer than 200 Jews remain in Marrakech. Several synagogues can still be visited, including **Bitton** (rue Touareg), **Bethel** and **Lazama** (36 Derb Ragraga; Sun–Thur 9am–6pm, Fri 9am–1pm; tip expected). Several guides will offer to show you around for a tip. To the east is the well-kept Jewish cemetery of **Miâara** (Sun–Thur 7am–6pm, Fri 7am–3pm; donation expected), believed to date from the 17th century, and including 11 shrines of Jewish *marabouts* (holy men).

Badi Palace

Heading out of the southern side of the place des Ferblantiers you reach the towering walls of the **Badi Palace** ⑯ (daily 8.30–11.45am and 2.30–5.45pm; charge), recognisable from the many storks' nests that top the wall.

Ahmed el-Mansour came to the throne in 1578 after the Battle of the Three Kings – King Sebastian of Portugal and his Moroccan ally Abu Abdullah Mohammed II Saadi, who wanted to recover his throne from his uncle Abd Al-Malik

The former royal Badi Palace

Saadi. All three died in battle but the Portuguese were defeated and the Moroccans acquired great wealth from ransoms and captured treasures. Just five months after the battle, Ahmed el-Mansour Eddahbi started building this palace, which deserved its name 'the Incomparable', a very worldly use of one of the 99 names of Allah. In 1598 Ahmed el-Mansour captured Timbuktu and acquired so much wealth that he was given yet another title, ed-Dhabi or 'the Golden'. The king employed the best craftsmen and bought the finest materials. It is said that he exchanged Italian marble for Moroccan sugar from the Souss Valley, pound for pound, and that his quest for precious materials went as far as China. Walls and ceilings were covered with gold from Timbuktu, sunken gardens were filled with perfumed flowers, the central pool was 90m (300ft) long with an island in the middle: everything was as lavish as it could be.

The palace took 25 years to build, and although it was finished only a few months before al-Mansour's death in 1603, he threw plenty of extravagant parties and celebrations for the inauguration. Allegedly, when the old sultan asked his joker what he thought of the palace, the fool answered that it would make a big pile of stones if it were demolished. Little did he know that 90 years later Moulay Ismail would destroy the palace, and that it would take him 12 years to strip all its precious materials. He built himself a fine palace in Meknes with the 'big pile of stones'. Moulay Ismail did a definitive job, and visitors must use their imagination to envisage the splendour of what was one of the most magnificent palaces ever constructed.

The palace's **central courtyard** is massive, with five basins and four sunken gardens planted with orange trees. They would have been typical Moorish gardens with cypresses, palms, olive trees and perfumed flowers as well as citrus trees. On each side of the courtyard was a pavilion. The largest on the western side was the **Koubba el-Hamsiniya** (Pavilion of 50 Columns) and opposite it the Crystal Pavilion. To the north was the **Green Pavilion**, and south the **Koubba Khaysuran**, named after the sultan's favourite wife and now an exhibition space for local artists. In the northeastern corner a staircase gives access to the rooftop terrace with great views over the vastness of the complex and the rest of the medina.

Storks nesting on Badi Palace

The Minbar
The 12th-century *minbar* (stepped pulpit) of the

Koutoubia Mosque, a marvel of medieval Islamic art, is on display in an annex in the southeastern corner. It was built in Córdoba for an Almoravid mosque, but after destroying that building the conquering Almohad rulers moved it into an enclosure in their new mosque. After this mosque was found to be incorrectly directed towards Mecca and destroyed, the *minbar* was moved to the Koutoubia Mosque. In 1996 a US-led team worked on the conservation of the masterpiece, moving it to the Badi Palace. Originally every bit of surface was covered with carved wooden panels and intricate marquetry, of which some of the 1.3 million pieces were tinier than a grain of rice. All were clearly carved by the greatest masters of the time.

Today the Badi palace is used as a venue for the annual Marrakech Popular Arts Festival and during the International Film Festival (see page 96).

Detail in El-Bahia Palace

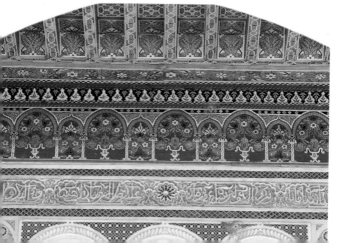

El-Bahia Palace

North of the place des Ferblantiers are two parallel streets that both run to the Jemaa el-Fna. These are the **rue Riad Zitoun el-Kedim** (Street of the Old Olive Grove) and **rue Riad Zitoun el-Jdid** (Street of the New Olive Grove). The first street starts off with shops selling interesting picture frames and small pieces of furniture

A courtyard in El Bahia

made from recycled car tyres, and becomes a budget hotel haven when it gets closer to Jemaa el-Fna. Rue Riad Zitoun el-Kedim is lined with a mixture of traditional Moroccan stalls, selling everything from carpets to kaftans, a scattering of western-run boutiques and some small antiques shops.

At the top of rue Riad Zitoun el-Jdid, on the corner, is another palace, **El-Bahia** ⑰ or 'the Brilliant' (Sat–Thur 8.45–11.45am and 2.45–5.45pm, Fri 8.45–11.30am and 3–5.45pm; charge). El-Bahia was built by two generations of 19th-century grand viziers, a ranking similar to prime minister. Si Moussa, who started building in the 1860s, was grand vizier to Sultan Sidi Mohammed ben Abdehrahman, and his son, the cruel Bou Ahmed, served Sultan Moulay Hassan and was regent for the child sultan Abdul Aziz. Sultan Abdul Aziz is said to have become so jealous of his vizier's fortunes that when Bou Ahmed died, he forced the family, who included four wives and 24 concubines, to leave. When the staff started stripping the palace, the sultan stopped them, only to collect all the booty for himself.

The Bahia Palace extends over 8 hectares (20 acres), and its complicated plan included a series of courtyards, gardens,

Storks are meant to bring good luck

pavilions and 150 rooms. One can almost smell the intrigue that must have been rife here.

The infamous warlord Madani Glaoui lived here from 1908 until 1911, when it became the residence of the French Résident-Général under the Protectorate.

Only part of the empty palace can be visited, as some of it is still used by the current royal family and their guests. King Mohammed VI once threw a lavish party here for the rapper P. Diddy.

Museum Street

Further north along rue Riad Zitoun el-Jdid, opposite the small parking area, are signs for two interesting museums, housed in grand *riads*. The **Dar Si Said Museum** ⑱ (Derb el Bahia, rue Riad Zitoun el Jedid; Wed–Mon 9am–noon and 3–6pm; charge) is in a modest palace built by Si Said, the brother of Bou Ahmed. The building, which was turned into a museum in the 1950s, is small and has some gorgeous painted ceilings and fine woodwork. The museum houses an important collection of decorative arts and crafts from the south of the country as well as the occasional exhibition of modern art. The room closest to the entrance is lined with some beautiful wooden doors rescued from kasbahs and old medina houses.

Further along is the oldest item in the museum's collection: a fine 10th-century marble fountain basin brought to Marrakech from Córdoba. Near the courtyard stands an ancient-looking ferris wheel that was used to entertain children during saints' festivals until the 1970s. Around the courtyard are rooms holding rich displays of southern Moroccan jewellery, with filigree silver from the Jbel Siroua, fibules from Tiznit and ornate powder horns and daggers. Also interesting is the carpet collection. The Berber carpets, or *hanbels*, are more colourful and employ mainly geometric patterns; those made by the Arab tribes, in dark reds and purples, have more chaotic designs and are traditionally narrower as they were made to fit their tents. The last room contains some exquisite carved cedar woodwork, some rescued from the Badi palace.

Nearby is **Maison Tiskiwine** ⑲ (8 rue de la Bahia; daily 9am–12.30pm and 3–5.30pm; charge), the private house and collection of long-time Marrakech resident, the Dutch anthropologist Bert Flint. He has collected tribal art for decades and has organised the exhibition geographically as a journey along the old trade routes between Marrakech and Timbuktu. He is passionate about his mission to point out that Marrakech is more African than Arabic in its roots, and he illustrates here the city's strong historic link with Timbuktu. The museum is compelling, with displays of colourful and fine pottery, jewellery, textiles and carpets. You can envisage what it was like to be a trader, travelling in one of the camel caravans and encountering different tribes on the way. The journey ends in Timbuktu, represented by Flint's peaceful courtyard filled with birdsong.

Sacred storks

In Moroccan culture storks, which are often seen nesting on rooftops, minarets and walls, are considered a sign of good fortune. Berbers believe that storks are transformed humans. In *The Garden of Secrets*, the Spanish writer Juan Goytisolo alludes to this belief, and tells the story of the Stork-Man.

GUÉLIZ AND HIVERNAGE

When the French arrived early in the 20th century and made Morocco their Protectorate, they turned up their noses at the native quarters of the walled medina and decided to build their new town, as elsewhere in Morocco, outside the walls. This *ville nouvelle* was elegant, with wide avenues and large villas surrounded by gardens and serene parks. Later on, wealthy Moroccans moved out of the medina as well, into apartments and houses in the new town. In the 1970s most visitors stayed in Guéliz as the medina was too much of a hassle, but that changed in the 1990s when people started renovating *riads*, transforming them into guesthouses. These are almost always the most charming places to stay, and provide a unique insight into this traditional Moroccan way

New shopping centre and apartments on Marrakech Plaza, Guéliz

of living. For those who prefer not to delve into the medieval medina, however, Guéliz and Hivernage offer an increasingly good selection of more western-style hotels.

Café in Guéliz

The new town divides into Guéliz, the lively area centred on avenue Mohammed V, and the quieter Hivernage, which has plenty of large villas and hotels. The *ville nouvelle* has a wealth of colonial architecture, a cosmopolitan atmosphere and offers visitors a chance to escape the narrow alleys and souks for Western-style shopping, varied international dining, art galleries and nightlife.

Guéliz

The 3km (2-mile) -long broad avenue that runs right through Marrakech, from the Koutoubia Mosque to the Jbel Guéliz (Mount Guéliz), is the buzzing **avenue Mohammed V**. About 400m/yds west of the Koutoubia Mosque is the **Ensemble Artisanal**, where craftsmen, including lantern makers, leather workers, woodworkers, weavers and jewellers, have workshops and sell their goods, perhaps at a slightly higher but fixed price. It's a good place to get an idea of price and quality before you start bargaining in the souks. On the opposite side of the road is the **Cyber Parc** (see page 67). There are three major roundabouts along Avenue Mohammed V: the **place de la Liberté** with a large fountain, the **place du 16 Novembre**, the heart of Guéliz, with the main post office, and the **place Abdelmoumen**

Théâtre Royal

Ben Ali lined by café terraces, the most popular of which is the **Café des Négociants**.

Just west of the place de la Liberté is the Eglise des Saints-Martyrs de Marrakech ⑳ (rue el-Imam, Guéliz; services Mon–Sat 6.30pm, Sun 10am), the *église* (church) from which Guéliz took its name. It was built in 1930 by the French, and dedicated to five 13th-century Franciscan friars who were beheaded in Muslim Seville for preaching Christianity. The stark, impressive facade translates into a cool spacious interior, decorated only by the sunlight streaming through the coloured stained glass.

Nearby, off the place du 16 Novembre, is the **Jnane el-Harti**, a small park originally laid out by the French as a formal garden and zoo. This is a popular place for an early evening stroll. Further west is the splendid **Théâtre Royal** (avenue de France; daily 8.30am–7pm; free) inaugurated in 2001. Designed by one of Morocco's leading architects, Charles Boccara, it has a classical portico and dome, and an auditorium linked by a courtyard to the 1,200-seat open-air theatre. The theatre is only sporadically used, but exhibitions by local and visiting artists fill the exhibition hall.

Most of the up-market shopping and trendy restaurants are around the **place Abdelmoumen Ben Ali** and what was the old **Marché Central** (Central Market) which was controversially destroyed and moved into a lesser building on rue Ibn Toumert, behind the huge **Marrakech Plaza** ㉑ on place du 16 Novembre – a fountain-filled space bordered with

European shops and Café 16, one of the best places for *patis-serie* or an alfresco lunch. Nearby is **Grand Café de la Poste**, a lovely French brasserie and one of the chicest places to eat, drink and hang out, all set inside one of the few remaining colonial buildings in Guéliz.

Dozens of restaurants fill the streets leading off place du 16 Novembre and there are also several good bars, notably the Bab Hotel (corner of boulevard el Mansour Eddhabi and rue Mohammed el Beqal), the Sky Bar of the Hotel la Renaissance (corner of boulevard Mohammed V and boulevard Mohammed Zerktouni), African Chic (rue Oum Errabia) which has live music, and l'Apero, on rue Abou Hayane Taouhidi. This stretch of avenue Mohammed V, as

Art Galleries

Guéliz is scattered with some superb art galleries. The **Matisse Art Gallery** (61 rue de Yougoslavie, No. 43 Passage Ghandouri) show-cases the talents of the next generation of Moroccan artists. **Galerie Ré** (Residence Al Andalus III, Corner of rues de la Mosquée and Ibn Toumert) mixes innovative painting, sculpture, photography and instal-lations from Morocco, Europe and the Middle East. **Galerie Tindouf** (22 boulevard Mohammed VI) has a collection of rare Fassi ceramics, precious textiles, Indian miniatures, Islamic calligraphy and 19th-century French Orientalist painting. **Galerie 127** (127 avenue Mohammed V, 2nd floor) has exhibitions by mostly French and Moroccan photogra-phers. The **David Bloch Gallery** (8 rue Vieux Marrakchi) celebrates street art in particular, and **Galerie Noir Sur Blanc** (48 rue de Yougoslavie, 1st floor) is a dynamic space with monthly exhibitions and cultural activities. The **Galerie Lawrence Arnott** (Immeuble el Khalil, avenue Hassan II) is devoted to more traditional art with figu-rative paintings by Moroccan and European artists, including Jacques Majorelle and Hamri.

Hivernage

well as the area around the **rue de Yougoslavie** and **rue de la Liberté** – both of which are lovely shopping streets with numerous boutiques – has numerous examples of colonial 'Mauresque' architecture.

The small **Spanish Quarter** just west of the rue de Yougoslavie, with diverse, colourful single-storey cottages, is all that is left of the large Spanish population that once lived here. North of boulevard Mohammed Zerktouni is another reminder of colonial days, the large **European Cemetery ㉒** (rue Er-Rouada; Apr–Sept 7am–7pm, Oct–Mar 8am–6pm; free), which dates from the 1920s. The overgrown cemetery, a romantic and peaceful place that is rarely visited, contains the tombs of the *colons*, overgrown with wild flowers and shaded by towering palm trees. A white obelisk reminds visitors of the soldiers who died in North Africa fighting to free France during World War II, an episode recounted in the film Days of Glory (2006). A few minutes' walk eastwards is the delightful **Majorelle Gardens** (see page 65).

Hivernage

South of Guéliz, **Hivernage** was built as an intimate garden suburb, with large villas surrounded by greenery. Stroll around the narrow winding streets and have a drink in the area's oldest hotel, the **Es Saadi**. Several popular bars include Le Comptoir, Jad Mahal, Theatro, Silver and La Suite (see page 88). Further west lie the large, pleasant **Menara Gardens** (see page 64).

GARDENS

Gardens are hugely important in Islamic culture, as they are thought to be the earthly realisation of paradise as it is described in the Qur'an. Large royal gardens and small internal courtyard gardens alike are places full of shade, birdsong, perfume, beauty and pleasure, but they are also considered to be places where heaven meets earth, infinity meets the temporary and God and mankind come into contact.

Marrakech has often been described as a huge palm grove, as a garden with surprisingly lush vegetation in a region with so little water. The secret behind the gardens and the Palmeraie (palm grove) was the water brought from the Atlas Mountains, or from underground water sources by *khettaras* (underground water channels) – a system the Moroccans borrowed from the ancient Persians, via the Arabs. The Palmeraie

Courtyard gardens are a place of serenity

and other gardens have suffered considerably in recent decades because of the city's rapid expansion, but still offer a tranquil respite from the heat and buzz of the city.

The Palmeraie

Marrakech's **Palmeraie** once spread over more than 13,000 hectares (32,000 acres), and it was estimated that it had about 150,000 palm trees, all watered by the *khettaras*. Legend has it that it was created by the date pips casually thrown aside by the Arab soldiers camping outside the city before conquering it.

The Palmeraie has undergone a lot of change in recent years. The *khettara* system no longer functions and water is provided by artesian wells, the date palms all over North Africa have suffered from a virus and, most significantly, large plots of land were sold off to build luxury hotels and large villas for wealthy Moroccans and foreigners. It is still, however, pleasant

Camel rides are available in the Palmeraie

to cycle through the winding lanes in the shade of palms, and camel rides are also on offer (tours depart from the Palmier D'Or), though the main attraction these days is to sit by a pool on a hot day.

Among many luxury places to stay, the beautiful **Jnane Tamsna** is set in a garden lovingly designed by the owner, ethno-botanist Gary Martin and his wife Meryanne Loum Martin. It

Agdal Gardens with the Atlas Mountains in the distance

offers a set menu lunch made from garden produce (see page 141). At the other end of the spectrum, the über-trendy **Nikki Beach** (see page 91) is another pleasant oasis, though slightly less peaceful. The Palmeraie is not called the 'Beverly Hills of Morocco' for nothing.

Agdal Gardens

Just south of the medina, the **Agdal Gardens** ❷❸ (Fri and Sun, 9am–sunset, closed if the king is in residence; free) was originally spread over 500 hectares (1,200 acres), more or less the same area as the entire medina. It was laid out by the Almohad rulers, at the back of the royal palace, in 1156. At the centre is a huge pool, the **Sahraj el-Hana** (The Tank of Health), in which the 19th-century Sultan Mohammed IV tragically drowned while rowing with his son. Around the pool are different kinds of orchards, including a palm grove, oranges, figs, pomegranates, vines and walnut trees, as well as several ornamental pavilions. You can climb onto the roof of the one beside the pool for a great view over the garden, set against the dramatic backdrop of the High Atlas Mountains.

Menara

The **Menara** ㉔ (avenue de la Ménara; daily 8.30am–sunset; free but charge for picnic pavilion) very much follows the plan of the quintessential Islamic garden, with orchards, pools and a pavilion. The gardens were designed by the Almohad sultan Abd al Mu'min during the 12th century, and have a central basin 200m (650ft) long and 150m (500ft) wide, fed by underground channels. The 16th-century pavilion was used by sultans for summertime escapes and romantic liaisons – legends tell of displeased sultans flinging their courtesans into the reservoir – and was restored by Moulay Abderrahman in the 19th century. It has one of the quintessential images of Marrakech – that of the pavilion, reflected in the pool and set against the backdrop of the High Atlas. There is a 'Sound and Light' show most evenings, though it is largely unimpressive – a simple stroll through the gardens early in

Majorelle Gardens

the morning or at sunset is far more picturesque.

Majorelle Gardens

The jewel in the crown of Marrakech gardens is the stunning, iconic **Majorelle Gardens** ㉕ (avenue Yaqoub el-Mansour; www.jardinmajorelle.com; daily Oct–late Apr 8am–5.30pm, May–late Sept 8am–6pm; charge).

Majorelle blue

Jacques Majorelle gave his name to the electric cobalt blue with which he painted the exterior of his studio, setting off the green of the garden perfectly. Some say it was inspired by the blue of French workmen's over-alls, others claim he was inspired by Berber homes in the south.

It was created in the 1930s by the French artist Jacques Majorelle, and purchased in 1980 by French fashion designer Yves Saint Laurent (who died in June 2008) and his partner Pierre Bergé.

Jacques Majorelle came to Marrakech in 1919 to recover from heart problems, and fell in love with the light and the colours. He bought the land in 1924 and designed an exotic botanical garden around his studio. The cactus garden has species from all over the world and looks monumental against the electric blue. Other features are the spectacular bougainvillea and a rustling bamboo forest, interspersed with pools filled with water lilies and lively with frogs. His studio houses a small **Islamic Museum**, with some of his own work, and a beautiful collection of Berber jewellery, magnificent carved doors and fine textiles. The studio also holds Saint Laurent's and Bergé's magnificent collection of Islamic art – ceramics, weapons, jewellery, textiles, carpets and woodwork – from the Maghreb, Africa and Asia, and some riveting photographs of Saint Laurent's glamorous life in Morocco in the 1970s, spanning over twenty years. There are also temporary exhibitions, the latest being a retrospective of Saint Laurent's Moroccan-inspired fashion.

The small **boutique** sells books, jewellery and good-quality crafts. The gardens are immensely popular so visit early in the morning or late afternoon. The small café in the garden serves a good breakfast until 11.30am as well as salads and snacks for lunch. There is a juice and salad bar (*Kaowa*) plus a cluster of elegant boutiques on the street outside the entrance.

La Mamounia

The grand dame of Marrakech, **La Mamounia** (avenue Bab Jdid, southern medina; www.mamounia.com) is one of the most famous hotels in the world, 'the Dorchester of North Africa' and, once upon a time, the life and soul of Marrakech. The grounds date back to the 18th century, when the Alaouite sultan Sidi Mohammed Ben Abdullah gave the gardens as a wedding gift to his son, Mamoun, who used them for glamorous parties. La Mamounia opened as a hotel in 1923 – a dazzling example of superior Moroccan craftsmanship and elegant Art Deco design.

The hotel reopened in 2010 after an ambitious three-year, multi-million dollar redesign. But you don't have to stay here to get a hit. Come for afternoon tea and afterwards wander around the spectacular gardens. Two hundred year-old olives as tall as oak trees tower over immaculate lawns and scented gardens bursting with roses, Barbary figs, Madagascar periwinkles, amaranths and agaves. Winston Churchill, a regular guest, thought it was 'the loveliest spot in the whole world.' There is also an organic vegetable garden with peach, orange, fig and

Fountain in Hotel La Mamounia

lime trees and everything here is used at the three Michelin-supervised restaurants – 'L'Italien', 'Le Français' and 'Le Marocain'. Alternatively, there is the slightly more relaxed 'Le Pavillon de la Piscine', which is open for breakfast and lunch.

The Cyber Parc

Just north of the Koutoubia and squeezed between the city walls and Avenue Mohammed V, the **Cyber Parc** ㉖ is another popular and attractive public garden. Owned in the 18th century by Moulay Abdel Salam, an Alaouite prince and poet, this beautiful park was brought into the 21st century

The Cyber Parc

by the Mohammed VI Foundation for the Protection of the Environment to give the medina more green space. The 8-hectare (20-acre) grounds highlight typical local vegetation: olive groves and orchards intermingle with water features and contemporary areas with grasses and flowers. In an unusual meeting of tradition and innovation, the gardens have at their centre a good internet service (internet café and Wi-fi hotspots).

EXCURSIONS FROM MARRAKECH

One of the great sights in Marrakech, visible from November to May, is the backdrop of the snowy peaks of the magnificent High Atlas mountains.

The most obvious escape is towards the Ourika Valley for a picnic or a walk, or a swim in **Lake Lalla Takerkoust**, and in winter there is the option of skiing in **Oukaimeden**. The **High Atlas** offers endless opportunities for hiking, horse riding or visiting weekly rural souks, and to the east of Marrakech are the famous **Cascades d'Ouzoud** (waterfalls). For a breath of fresh sea air, escape to the enchanting seaside village of **Essaouira**.

A range of hotels and guesthouses outside Marrakech offer sports activities in the surrounding countryside, country clubs and private pools attract sun seekers and the mountains offer numerous possibilities to escape the city.

Lake Lalla Takerkoust and Ourika Valley

The artificial **Lake Lalla Takerkoust ㉗**, formed by the dam built by the French between 1929 and 1935 to provide

Ourika Valley

Marrakech with electricity, is only 40km (25 miles) away. The lake is a picturesque escape, set against the High Atlas, and has several restaurants and guesthouses around it – the best being Le Flouka and Le Relais du Lac. This is a popular summer excursion and there are several refreshing options for cooling down in the water, as well as swimming: pedal boats, kayaks, windsurf boards and even jet skis.

South of Marrakech and about 20km (12 miles) east of the lake is the beautiful **Ourika Valley** ㉖. The temperature in summer is far more agreeable here and the river banks are a popular spot in summer for picnicking or camping. It is a good place to go for the day, or spend a few days trekking.

The Ourika Road (P2017) leads south of Marrakech to the Ourika Valley, and after 34km (21 miles) is the village of **Tnine-l'Ourika**, which has a great souk on Mondays. Signposted from the village is La Safranière (www.safran-ourika.com; daily 8am–6pm; charge), which offers guided tours of the farm where the purple flowers of the *Crocus sativus*, which originally came from Kashmir and Nepal, produce excellent saffron. The plants only flower for 20 days a year, usually the first three weeks of November, and 140 flowers are needed to produce 1 gram of saffron.

Nearby, in the same village is **Nectarome** (www.nectarome.com; daily Mar–July and Sept 9am–7pm, Oct–Feb 9am–5pm; charge) where 50 different plants are grown for the production of organic essential oils and bath products, which are for sale in the shop. You can visit alone or with a guided tour (1–1.5 hours) and lunch can be made on request.

Run by the same people who own the Maison de la Photographie in Marrakech, the **Ecomusée Berbère** (www. ecomuseeberbere.com; Tue–Sun 9.30am–7pm, charge) is situated in a traditional *pisé* building that dates back to the early 20th century. With the help of the local people, the museum has been filled with a collection of carpets, jewellery, clothing and pottery. There is an exhibit of hundreds of old photographs and documentaries on the world of the Berbers. The museum also organizes walks into the countryside, visits to pottery workshops and farms.

From Tnine l'Ourika the Ourika river winds through orchards, gardens and fields, with great views of picturesque *douars* (tiny *pisé* villages). At the lovely village of **Aghbalou**, the road divides in two with the left turn going to **Setti**

Selling mint in Tnine-l'Ourika

Fatma and the right to the ski and trekking resort of **Oukaïmeden.**

Setti Fatma ㉙ is a pretty village with many opportunities for trekking. The most popular option is the walk to the **Seven Waterfalls**, about four hours away, for a swim and a picnic, but for longer treks contact the **Bureau des Guides** in the village.

Snowy peaks of Jbel Toubkal

Oukaïmeden ㉚, 75km (46 miles) south of Marrakech, is Africa's highest ski station at 2,600m (8,500ft). The season, if there is snow, runs roughly from late December to the end of March and the pistes range from nursery to a black run. There is little in the way of piste grooming so conditions can be rough and skiing off-piste is inadvisable. There are six button lifts and one chair lift – the highest in North Africa, at 3,243 metres – to the top of **Jbel Oukaïmeden**. A viewpoint with an orientation table is set at the top, with views south to Toubkal and northwards to Marrakech. There are pre-historic rock engravings along the north side of the plateau. Skis and boots can be hired from the bottom of the piste and a French chalet-style restaurant and guesthouse, Chez Juju, is very popular for lunch. For the rest of the year Oukaïmeden is a good base for walking.

High Atlas

The wildest place to visit from Marrakech is undoubtedly the **Toubkal National Park** in the **High Atlas**. The road up to Asni is at first uneventful but soon becomes dramatic, with superb views of the fertile river valley and mud-brick villages clinging to the hillside. **Asni** ㉛ is the first main village along

Kasbah du Toubkal eco-lodge

the road, 47km (29 miles) south of Marrakech. It is a Berber village, famous for its large **Saturday souk**, which attracts tour groups from Marrakech. A spectacular road leads through deep gorges and lush mountain scenery to **Imlil** ㉜, 17km (10 miles) away. Imlil is the main starting point for climbing North Africa's highest peak, Jbel Toubkal (4,167m/13,666ft), a popular two- to four-day climb. The village is well set up with a **Bureau des Guides**, where you can hire guides and arrange treks and ascents of the mountain (see page 93), as well as restaurants, souvenir stalls and shops to stock up on food. A good day walk is to **Aremd** (1 hour from Imlil) and another 1.5 hours to **Sidi Chamarouch** at 2,600m (8,500ft), the shrine of the saint of the same name.

Many visitors from Marrakech head for the **Kasbah du Toubkal** (www.kasbahdutoubkal.com), just above the village of Imlil. This wonderful eco-lodge is the brainchild of Mike McHugo and a group of local Berbers. The former summer lodge of the local *caid* (ruler) has spectacular views over the surrounding mountains, and is a place of serenity and retreat. Lunch, served on the rooftop terrace in good weather, is a simple Berber-style meal. The lodge has luxurious rooms, a *hammam*, and dormitories for students, but many people just go for lunch and a short walk into the surrounding countryside.

Back towards Asni, and continuing further south along the main road, is the village of **Ouirgane** ㉝ (60km/37 miles from Marrakesh), in the middle of the lush foothills of the

Atlas. Ourigane is a quiet village and a good base for treks into the surroundings. It also has a souk on Thursdays and some lovely places to have lunch or spend the day by a pool, such as La Bergerie, La Roseraie and L'Oliveraie. The Auberge Sanglier Qui Fume has cosy accommodation and is very popular for lunch as well as offering *petanque*, a pool, billiards and mountain biking.

The N10, which continues towards the **Tizi-n-Test**, is one of the most beautiful – and vertiginous – roads in Morocco. After Ouirgane the road enters the **N'Fis Gorges** then follows the **Agoundis River** valley, dotted by **kasbahs** that belonged to the powerful Goundafa Berber tribe who controlled this region in the 19th century. Forty kilometres (25 miles) after Ouirgane, commanding the area high up on the opposite river bank is the splendid **mosque of Tin-Mal** 34 (daily; charge). The 12th-century mosque is all that remains of the Almohad city of Tin-Mal, and it is one of only two mosques non-Muslims can enter in Morocco. Built in 1156 in honour of the Almohad spiritual leader, Mohammed ibn Toumert, the mosque is austere yet beautiful. Climb to the top of the minaret for wonderful views over the valley. If the door is closed a guardian can usually be found to let you in.

Cascades d'Ouzoud

Cascades d'Ouzoud

The **Cascades d'Ouzoud** ㉟ (Ouzoud Falls), 165km (100 miles) northeast of Marrakech, are a popular day trip for Marrakchis, who come for picnics and to enjoy the cooling waters of Morocco's biggest waterfall. The water of the Oued Ouzoud (River of Olives) plunges down 110m (360ft) in three main tiers and into an idyllic pool overlooked by souvenir stalls and terraced cafés serving *tagines* and drinks. The falls are most spectacular between March and June. The place gets busy at weekends and in summer when students camp nearby, but for most of the year it is easy to see the appeal of this place, which is like a perfect image of paradise hidden deep in the Atlas mountains. Views of the falls from above are beautiful, but walk down to the bottom for the full effect. The currents make it dangerous to swim in the plunge pool, but it is delightful to do so in the pools downstream.

Those with itchy feet can go for a walk, following the river downstream about 3km (2 miles) to the photogenic old Berber village of **Tanaghmelt**, which seemingly blends into the hillside; or for a longer walk 20km (12 miles) upstream to the Gorges of el-Abid, with about 15 smaller cascades, pools and beaches on the way. The charming **Riad Cascades d'Ouzoud** (www.ouzoud.com; see page 142) arranges longer treks in the area, as well as kayaking and abseiling in the dry canyons.

An extra attraction, particularly for children, are the large groups of Barbary apes who play and live around the

Essaouira locals

Explore the art galleries in Essaouira

falls, and who chase each other on the surrounding rocks, seemingly for the sole entertainment of tourists. The easiest way to get to the falls is by your own transport; otherwise take the bus from Marrakech to Azilal and then a *grand taxi*. If you do have your own car, stop en route at **Demnate**, a lively walled town, with a wonderful **Sunday souk**, famous for olives and local pottery.

Essaouira

The white and windy city of **Essaouira 36**, 175km (110 miles) west of Marrakech, is one of the most attractive cities along Morocco's Atlantic coast. With its year-round mild temperatures, long history and leisurely pace it has always attracted artists and writers, and now also appeals to those escaping the Marrakech buzz. The town can be visited on a day trip, but to do the place justice and to feel the full attraction, you need to stay at least one night. The charming blue

Barbary apes

Barbary apes or macaques (*Macaca sylvanus*) live in forests in Morocco, north Algeria and Gibraltar, but they are at high risk of extinction. An Italian primatologist found that the population has declined dramatically from 40,000 to 6,000 in the last two decades.

and white medina has a few sights but the main pleasure is to stroll around the narrow streets, explore the art galleries for which Essaouira is renowned and the colourful souks (less hectic than those in Marrakech), watch the fishing boats come in, sit on a café terrace to watch the world go by, or enjoy the wild windswept beach, famous now for its superb kite- and windsurfing.

Depending on who you ask, the name *Es-Saouir* has two extremely different meanings, either 'the little ramparts' or 'the beautifully designed'. The town was also known in history as both Amougdoul and Mogador, names that probably go back to its Phoenician origins in the 7th century BC – *migdol* in Phoenician means lookout tower. The Phoenicians extracted the precious purple dye from the murex shells they found on the Île de Mogador, just off the mainland. The town as it looks today is entirely the work of Sultan Sidi Mohammed ben Abdullah, who in 1760 hired the Frenchman Théodore Cornut to design the city, and the walls, of his chosen naval basis.

The port kept growing in importance until the early 19th century, and the town amassed incredible wealth, mostly because of the role of the large Jewish community. There were 17,000 Jews here, compared to fewer than 10,000 Muslims, and they had a special status as the middlemen between the Sultan and the foreign traders. Essaouira was the port for Timbuktu (now in Mali), and European goods such as Manchester cotton were exchanged here for African gold, salt, sugar, ivory and gum arabic.

By the 20th century the trade had dwindled, because the local Berber chieftains were more interested in arms deals and ransoms than in trading goods, and because most Jewish families had left. The French Protectorate chose Casablanca as its commercial centre. In the 1960s Essaouira became a favourite hippy hang-out, attracting musicians like Cat Stevens and Jimi Hendrix, as well as director Orson Welles, who shot his film *Othello* here. Then the surfers came, drawn by the huge waves and strong winds that give the town the title of 'Windy City of Africa'. In recent years they have been joined by house-buying Europeans.

The Medina and the Port

The picturesque old medina was declared a Unesco World Heritage site in 2001. The only way to explore the winding alleys of the medina is by foot and the best place to start is the

Mending nets by the ramparts in Essaouira

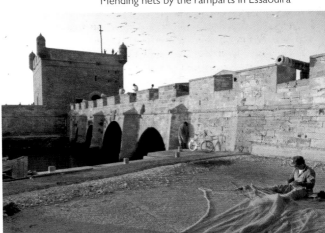

Thuya wood

Essaouira is famous for its thuya woodwork, which comes from a thuya forest nearby – one of the only places in the world where the thuya tree grows. The *racines* (roots) of the tree provide a rich texture with knots, while the *tiges* (branches) give a lovely stripey pattern to dense chestnut-coloured wood.

picturesque **place Moulay el-Hassan Ⓐ**. There are several cafés and restaurants lining the square, which becomes a lively gathering place in the evenings and along the main street leading off it, which has several good places for lunch or a coffee, notably Café France and Gelateria Dolce Freddo.

On place Moulay Hassan itself is a restaurant/bar called Casa Vera, which has a roof terrace with fantastic views over the port (and an alcohol licence). Between the square and the port are one of Essaouira's main eating attractions – the **grilled fish stalls** serving freshly caught fish and seafood. Past the *grillades* is the port, a vibrant place to wander around, particularly in the afternoons when the fishing boats bring in their catch. In the middle of it all is Chez Sam, an Essaouira institution, and an atmospheric place to eat in the heart of the port.

Essaouira's main souk streets lie behind place Moulay el Hassan in avenue de l'Istiqual and avenue Sidi Mohammed Ben Abdellah. Between avenue Oqba ibn Nafi and place Moulay el Hassan you will find an enclave of carpet and kaftan shops and, on Place Chefchaouni, a peaceful café. The **ramparts Ⓑ**, called the *skala* (reached via rue de la Skala, off place Moulay Hassan), are one of Essaouira's main attractions. European cannons, several of British manufacture, were gifts from the merchants to the Sultan Mohammed ben Abdellah. Promenade en Mer (tel: 0524-47 46 18) runs daily boat trips around the islands, offering a close up view for enthusiasts of the islands' abundant bird life.

In the carpenters' souk beneath the ramparts, craftsmen carve everything from small items such as boxes, bracelets and picture frames to large chess sets, tables and cabinets out of thuya and cedar wood. One of the finest woodworkers' souks in Morocco, it supplies shops and bazaars all over the country and abroad. The Ensemble Artisanal, showcasing local crafts, is quartered in the turreted Borj de Marrakech on the southwestern corner of the ramparts, behind the Hotel des Isles.

Mellah and Markets

Past the museum, at the crossroads, rue Sidi Mohammed ben Abdullah leads up to the narrow dark alleys of the old Jewish quarter (Mellah). Only three or four Jewish families still live here – many left for Israel long ago – and the area was falling apart until foreigners recently began buying houses.

Shop selling items made from thuya wood

From the **Bab Doukkala** at the end of the Mellah, the avenue Zerktouni, the city's main street, leads back to the harbour. On the right-hand side is the **Souk Jdid**, the main vegetable, fruit and fish markets, surrounded by spice shops. On the opposite side of the road is the old **Marché de Grain ⊙** (Grain Market), which now has several pleasant cafés and some interesting shops. The street continues to the tree-lined **avenue Oqba ben Nafia**, the old *méchouar* (assembly place or processional avenue), with the splendid pink city walls. Several art galleries have opened, selling the colourful work of local Essaouira artists. The **Damgaard Gallery ⊙**, just off place Orson Welles, has been exhibiting works by Essaouira's famous painters since 1988. On 4 rue de Tetouan is **Galerie la Kasbah ⊙**, set in an 18th-century *riad*, Galerie l'Arbre Bleu is on 233 rue Chbanate and on 20 rue Malek ben al Morhal a young artist, Youssef el Qaouatli,

Fishing boats jostle for space in the port

shows and sells his work in his home. The **Afalkay Art Gallery** (9 place Prince Moulay El Hassan) is dedicated to woodcarving and has some beautiful thuya wood exhibits.

The **Museum of Sidi Mohammed ben Abdallah** ❻ (9am–6pm, closed Tue; charge) in rue Laalouj is worth a visit for its collection

Fish stall with the day's catch

of jewellery, musical instruments and costumes documenting the cultural heritage of Essaouira and the region.

Along the Boulevard Mohammed V, running from the medina to the end of the beach, there are several good beach restaurants, the most popular of which is the Chalet de la Plage, as well as some of the town's more upmarket hotel chains, including the Sofitel. At the end of the Boulevard are some lovely laid-back beach cafés – **Beach and Friends** and **Ocean Vagabond** are the best – as well as the well-organised **Club Mistral**, where surfboards, kites and windsurfs can be rented. On the beach outside Ocean Vagabond, horses and camels can be hired for rides down to the more deserted stretches. The **Ranch de Diabet** (tel: 0670-57 68 41) also arranges rides (horse and camel) on the beach, into the surrounding countryside and to historic sites. Quads can be hired from outside Ocean Vagabond and also from Quad Pro Isfaoun (tel: 0524-47 49 06), Sahara Quad (tel: 0673-44 95 41) and Palma Quad (tel: 0666-709 999).

At the farthest end of Essaouira's beach lies Diabet, a sleepy jumble of whitewashed houses made famous by a visit from Jimi Hendrix.

WHAT TO DO

SHOPPING

Marrakech is a shoppers' paradise: from the endless souks filled with Berber jewellery, kaftans, spices and carpets, to trendy boutiques in Guéliz or designer showrooms out in the Sidi Ghanem industrial zone, it has it all. Many of the shops in the souks sell similar wares, but venture off the well-trodden paths or check out the shops of new designers to find something bespoke.

Crafts

Unlike many other places in the world, Marrakech still produces many traditional crafts. It is said that if you can dream it up, someone somewhere in the medina can make it. Marrakech is deservedly famous for its leatherwork, from traditional poufs and saddle bags to travel bags, belts and sandals, ceramics and pottery, intricate metalwork and, of course, carpets.

Opening hours

The shops in the medina are usually open from 10am–8pm. Some close on Friday afternoon, and many are closed all day on Sunday. In Guéliz, shops are open from Monday to Saturday 10am–1pm and again from 4–7.30pm.

A good place to start looking for traditional crafts is at the government-run **Ensemble Artisanal** opposite the Cyber Parc. Craftsmen sell their traditional wares at fixed prices, so it is a good place to get an idea of what is available, before heading for the souks. The one-stop shop for furniture, lanterns, candlesticks, textiles, leather and some wonderful antiques is

Shop in a souk for colourful and exotic purchases

Mustapha Blaoui at 144 rue Bab Doukkala. **Kifkif** at 3 rue des Ksour, Bab Laksour, does a modern take on local crafts. **Al Kawtar**, 57 Rue Laksour, is a non-profit organization producing handmade, traditional Moroccan embroidery by disadvantaged women and girls. The best places for pottery are **Akkal**, 322 Sidi Ghanem Industrial Zone, and **Jamade**, Derb Riad Zitoune Kedim. For lanterns, head to place des Ferblantiers (see page 48) or Fondouk el Fatmi, Bab Fteuh.

Antiques and Carpets

Morocco has an endless variety of carpets and rugs. The dozens of stalls in the **Souk des Tapis** (Criée Berbère) are the place to go and **Bazaar du Sud**, at No 117, has a large selection. In Guéliz, **Galerie Tadghart** at 11 Immeuble Berdai, on the corner of avenue Hassan I and the place de la Liberté, has an exquisite collection of textiles and **Ben Rahal** (28 rue de la Liberté) has a good selection of vintage and new carpets. **L'Orientaliste**, 11 & 15 rue de la Liberté, has antiques as well as paintings, glassware and perfume. **Darkoum** (5 rue de la Liberté) has stunning furniture and textiles from Morocco, Africa and India. There are several antique dealers at the beginning of rue Dar el-Bacha and rue Sidi el-Yamani in the

Carpet buyers will be spoilt for choice

medina, but the most impressive is **El-Badii** (54 boulevard Moulay Rachid) in Guéliz. For a flea market that rivals anything in London, Paris or New York head to **Souk el-Khemis** at the northern tip of the medina.

Jewellery

The souks have everything from tourist tat to antique, often Jewish-made, Berber jewellery. Near place des Ferblantiers is the Grand Bijouterie **gold souk**, but the gold dowry jewellery is more likely to appeal to locals. For unusual jewellery from Morocco and sub-Saharan Africa go to **Boutique Bel Hadj**, on the first floor of the Fondouk Ourzazi on the Bab Fteuh. La Galerie (see page 37) has the popular **Stephanie Jewels**, which sells filigree gold jewellery. **Michéle Baconnier** on 6 rue Vieux Marrakchi has expensive but lovely pieces.

Clothes

At **Au Fil d'Or**, 10 Souk Smarine, there are fine kaftans, shirts and jackets for men and women. For chic traditional women's clothes, styled for Western women and made to measure, there is no better place than **Aya's** in Derb Jdid Bab Mellah, just off place des Ferblantiers. **La Maison du Kaftan**, 65 rue Sidi el-Yamami, has the widest selection of Moroccan clothing. Florence Taranne sells a chic and eclectic selection of African-Moroccan kaftans and accessories at **Kulchi** (1 rue des Ksour). The most luxuriously embroidered kaftans and throws, all

Carpets of Morocco

Urban carpets are influenced by the intricate designs of the Middle East. Berber carpets have abstract patterns and symbols telling the stories of a tribe. Creamy *shedwi* carpets of the Beni Ourain and Beni Mguild tribes are decorated with dark brown patterns. *Haouz* from the west have free-floating shapes and bright colours. *Kilims* are flat-woven with detailed geometric designs.

produced in India, are available from **Akbar Delights**, place Bab Fteuh, just off the Jemaa el-Fna. **Kaftan Queen**, 44 rue Tarik ibn Ziad in Guéliz, has one-off kaftans and dresses and **Michéle Baconnier** also has Moroccan and Indian-inspired women's clothing.

Shoes and Leather
Souk el-Kebir has plenty of leather goods for sale. One piece of advice: the camel leather weekend bags look great but sniff them before you buy, as it is very hard to get rid of the pungent smell. The **Souk des Babouches** has a great selection of the typical Moroccan slippers, which range from the very glamorous to the utilitarian brown, red or yellow varieties for men. **Lalla** in La Galerie, Souk Cherifia, is a popular shop where French designer Laetitia Trouillet sells her funky, locally-made handbags and other gems.

The Hand of Fatima icon is a recurrent theme in jewellery

In Guéliz the first stop for fine leather is 139 avenue Mohammed V where **Intensité Nomade** has international and local designer labels, and on the opposite corner, try **Place Vendome**. For Western-style shoes, the most popular place is **Atika** at 34 rue de la Liberté.

Books

There are only a few bookshops in Marrakech selling English-language books. The **Café du Livre**, at 44 rue Tarek Ibn Ziad in Guéliz, is the best. With new books on Morocco as well as second-hand fiction, it is also the perfect place for a quiet coffee or lunch.

Morocco bound

Marrakech, The Red City: The City Through Writers' Eyes Barnaby Rogerson and Stephen Lavington (eds) (Sickle Moon Books, 2003)
Hideous Kinky by Esther Freud (Penguin, 1992)
A Year in Marrakesh by Peter Mayne (Eland, 2002)
The Voices of Marrakesh by Elias Canetti (Marian Boyars, 2001)
Lords of the Atlas, The Rise and Fall of Glaoua 1893–1956 by Gavin Maxwell (Century Publishing, 1983)
The Last Storytellers: Tales from the Heart of Morocco by Richard Hamilton (I.B.Tauris, 2011)

The best selection of beautiful coffee table books, not necessarily in English, is at **ACR Librairie d'Art** at the end of the passageway at 55 boulevard Mohammed Zerktouni in Guéliz. In the medina there is a good bookstore in the courtyard of the **Musée de Marrakech**.

NIGHTLIFE AND ENTERTAINMENT

Shopping may be exhausting, but keep a little breath for the city's nightlife. Hot new clubs and bars pop up all the time, mostly in the new town, which has a more tolerant approach to alcohol. The best place to start the evening is on the **Jemaa el-Fna** which has food, music and entertainers (see page 28).

Bars

A lovely place for an evening cocktail in the medina is the **Kosybar** (place des Ferblantiers), which combines a Moroccan tea salon, a sushi bar and a rooftop lounge bar. The meeting place in the new town is the colonial-style **Grand Café de la Poste** just behind the main post office on avenue Mohammed V, with a large outdoor terrace and beautiful upstairs bar. **Le Comptoir** (rue Echchouhada, Hivernage; tel: 0524-43 77 02; www.comptoirmarrakech.com), is popular and chic with excellent food and stylish nightly belly dancing. Laidback **Kechmara** (3 rue de la Liberté; tel: 0524-42 25 32; www.kechmara.com) has a great roof terrace, live music and a DJ from Wednesday to Saturday nights. **African Chic** (6 rue Oum Errabia; tel: 0524-43 14 24) has unexpectedly good salsa and tango while opulent **Jad Mahal** (10 rue Harroun Errachid; tel: 0524-43 69 84) has live music most evenings. A little way

Musicians at Le Comptoir

outside town is trendy **Bo et Zin** (Douar Lahna; Route de l'Ourika 3.5km; tel: 0524-38 80 12), situated in a beautiful garden with a bar and excellent Asian food.

Nightclubs

With the arrival of Pacha, the city is acquiring an Ibiza-like reputation for nightlife. Most of the clubs are in Guéliz and Hivernage. **Pacha Marrakech** (Zone hôtelière d'Agdal,

Only traditional bars are still a male preserve

boulevard Mohammed VI; tel: 0524-38 84 00; www.pacha marrakech.com) is a large complex with restaurants, lounges and a large clubbing area where some of the world's best DJs turn the tables. The old theatre at the Saadi hotel has been converted into techno club **Teatro** (rue Ibrahim el Mazini; tel: 0664-86 03 39). **Montecristo** (20 Rue Ibn Aicha; tel: 0524-43 90 31) has several floors of music and dancing. **La Suite** (Hotel Le Méridien N'Fis, avenue Mohammed V; tel: 0524-42 07 00; www.suiteclub.ma) attracts an international crowd, as does **Silver** (10 rue Haroun Errachid; tel: 0524-42 35 37), where DJs spin techno and house. **So Night Lounge** (Sofitel, rue Haroun Errachid; tel: 0656-51 50 09) stages a mixture of live bands and house music.

Cultural Life

Most of the films screened in Marrakech are in French or Arabic, and foreign films are often dubbed. The best cinemas in town are **Le Colisée** (boulevard Mohammed Zerktouni, Guéliz) and **Mégarama** (boulevard Mohammed VI, behind Pacha). The **Institut Français** (Route de Targa; tel: 0524-44 69 30) shows arthouse French and North African films and the

Instituto Cervantes (boulevard Mohammed V, tel: 0524-42 20 55) has Spanish films and talks.

HAMMAMS AND SPAS

One of the best ways to relax is to go to a traditional *hammam* (Turkish bath). The **Hammam Dar el-Bacha** (20 rue Fatima Zohra) in the medina has separate times for men and women and is one of the oldest *hammams* in town. For a more upmarket but still traditional experience try **Les Bains de Marrakech** – reservation essential (2 Derb Sedra, Bab Agnaou; www.lesbainsdemarrakech.com). Many *riads* and hotels offer spa facilities, but some of the best are the **Beldi Country Club** just outside town (tel: 0524-38 39 50; www.beldicountry club.com) which is also a blissful place to have lunch by the

Riad El Fenn has a *hammam* and offers a range of beauty treatments.

pool, and **Palais Rhoul and Spa** in the Palmeraie (tel: 0524-32 94 94/95; www.palaisrhoul.com) where the *hammamiste* will scrub you, throw buckets of water, give you a massage and finish off by squeezing an orange over you. **Ksar Char Bagh**, also in the Palmeraie (tel: 0524-32 92 44; www.ksarcharbagh. com) with its marble *hammam* is equally decadent and if you feel like really splashing out, head to the award-winning spa at **La Mamounia** (tel: 0524-38 86 00; www.mamounia.com).

SPORTS

In addition to its exciting nightlife and fantastic shopping, Marrakech more than caters for sports enthusiasts and those who just want a break from the city.

Swimming Pools

Many hotels with larger pools let you use the pool if you have lunch or for a small charge, including **Jardins de la Koutoubia** (26 rue de la Koutoubia; tel: 0524-38 88 00), **Jardins de la Medina** (21 Derb Chtouka, Kasbah; tel: 0524-38 18 51), **Es Saadi** (rue Ibrahim el Mazini; tel: 0524-44 88 11) and **La Sultana** (403 rue de la Kasbah; tel: 0524-38 80 08). In the Palmeraie, **Nikki Beach** (Circuit de la Palmeraie; tel: 0663-51 99 92; www.nikkibeach.com/marrakech) has a day-long-party-by-the-pool experience. **Pacha** (see page 89) has a lovely pool with a restaurant for use during the day; and the **Beldi Country Club** (Route du Barrage, Cherifa; www.beldicountryclub.com) has two pools set in a stunning rose garden. Beautiful **Les Deux Tours** (see page 141) – architect Charles Boccara's old home – has a tranquil pool and good lunch opportunities.

Cycling

It is easy to get around town on a bike. Bikes can be rented by the hour or day. A half day is between 60–100Dhs. Good bikes can be rented on place de la Liberté opposite the pet-rol station, from **Maroc Deux Roues** (avenue Mohammed V, opposite Bab Nkob; tel: 0661-59 27 14) and from **Actions Sports Loisirs** (1 avenue Yaqoub el-Mansour, Apt 4; tel: 0661-240 145), which has a wider selection, more appropriate for getting further out of town.

Horse Riding

There are several good stables near Marrakech. **Les Cavaliers de l'Atlas** (tel: 0672-84 55 79; www.lescavaliersdelatlas.com) and the **Palmeraie Golf Palace** (Circuit de la Palmeraie, tel: 0524-36 87 04; www.pgpmarrakech.com) have horses and ponies most suitable for children. In the Agafay Desert, half an hour from Marrakech is La Pause (Douar Lmih Laroussiene, Commune Agafay; tel: 0661-30 64 94; www.

Ride camels in Marrakech's Palmeraie, or head to Ranch de Diabat near Essaouira

lapause-marrakech.com) from where you can ride Berber horses into the surrounding desert, have lunch and swim in the pool.

Trekking and Running

Serious runners could join the annual **Marrakech Marathon** (www.marathon-marrakech.com) and trekking options abound. **The Kasbah du Toubkal** (see page 72) is a popular destination for an easy mountain walk combined with lunch. Other destinations are the idyllic **Cascades d'Ouzoud** (see page 74), the **Lake Lalla Takerkoust** (see page 68) and the popular **Ourika Valley** (see page 69).

It is possible to devise your own hikes in the **Toubkal National Park**. Unless you are a very experienced mountain hiker, hire a local guide and pack mules and follow the standard routes. The price of services, accommodation and food may be negotiable when business is quiet. Good springboards are Imlil, Oukaimeden and Tabant.

Basic accommodation on hikes is found in mountain refuges (usually run by the Club Alpin Français; www.caf-maroc. com). Each year the Moroccan National Tourist Office (www. visitmorocco.com) publishes a free guide covering most of the mountain areas.

Golf

The oldest course in Morocco is the **Royal Golf de Marrakech** (Ancienne Route de Ouarzazate; tel: 0524-40 98 28; 18 holes, par 72). Founded by Pasha Glaoui in 1923, it has been played on by Winston Churchill, David Lloyd George and Eisenhower. Lessons and caddies available. Created by Robert Trent Jones in 1993 the 5 star **Palmeraie Golf Palace** (Circuit de la Palmeraie; tel: 0524-36 87 04; 18 holes, par 72) is a championship-length course extending over 100 hectares. The **Amelkis Golf Resort** (Route de Ourarzazate;

The Royal Golf club

tel: 0524-40 44 14; 18 holes, par 72) is known as one of the most technically challenging courses in Marrakech. Like the Amelkis, the **Samanah Country Club** (Route d'Amizmiz; tel: 0524-84 18 84) is a five-star 300 hectare resort, with an 18 hole, 6,800 metre, USGA standard par 72 golf course. Rates for all start at around 500Dh per day.

Hot Air Ballooning

You will need a clear winter's day for full effect, but a bird's-eye view of the 'Red City', the surrounding palm groves and the snow-clad Atlas could prove the most memorable part of your stay. **Ciel d'Afrique** (Imm. Ali, appt. 4, avenue Youssef ben Tachfine; tel: 052443 28 43; www.cieldafrique. info) has been established for 20 years and you can take VIP flights where you have the balloon to yourself and are served champagne. **Marrakech By Air** (185 Lalla Haya Targa; tel: 0524-49 07 99; www.marrakechbyair.com) offers a similar service. On landing, you are met by the ground crew who set up a tent with a view of the Atlas and serve a traditional breakfast.

CHILDREN'S MARRAKECH

Moroccans love children and most children love Morocco. Check when booking a *riad* that the place is suitable for children. Family-friendly restaurants include **Chez Chegrouni** (see page 107), **Catanzaro** (see page 110), **Casanova** and the **stalls at Jemaa el-Fna**. Children will love the large selection of excellent ice creams at **Oliveri** (9 boulevard Mansour ed-Dahbi, tel: 0524-44 89 13; daily 10am–11pm).

Watching snake charmers, acrobats and musicians in the **Jemaa el-Fna** is fascinating. Kids love walking in the **souks** buying little souvenirs, and holding the **chameleons** in the spice shops of the Rahba Kedima.

Oasiria (4km along Route du Barrage; tel: 0524-38 04 38; www.oasiria.com; daily 10am–6pm; charge, free shuttle bus from Marrakech) is a large water park with all the usual facilities. Horse riding (see page 92) is a fine way to end the afternoon, as is camel riding – rides can be taken in the Palmeraie, from the Palmier d'Or, and from just outside the Menara Gardens. **La Pause** also has camel and horse rides, as well as crazy golf. **Kawkab Jeux** play park in Guéliz (1 rue Imam Chafaï, Kawkab Centre Harti; tel: 05 24 43 89 29; www.kawkab-jeux.com) has a fun kids' play area.

Snake charmers on
Jemaa el-Fna

Calendar of Events

The best place to find information on events is at the Tourist Office (see page 132) and in the *Marrakech Tribune*, published quarterly and available free at many *riads* and restaurants, or for sale at kiosks.

The month of Ramadan is the Muslim month of fasting, when local people abstain from food, drink, smoking and sex from sunrise to sunset. Many restaurants and bars are shut during the day, but at night the city celebrates. Islamic holidays are based on the lunar calendar.

January: *The Marrakech Marathon* (www.marathon-marrakech.com) is run by more than 5,000 Moroccan and foreign athletes through the medina and the Palmeraie.

February: *AiM (Arts in Marrakech) Biennale* (www.aimbiennale.org) has exhibitions, lectures, workshops and events throughout the city.

March: The *Marrakech International Magic Festival* (www.magiemarrakech.com) has performances by international magicians, mainly at the Royal Theatre. *Riad Art Expo* (www.riadart-expo.com) is a large design, interiors, gardening, gastronomy and lifestyle show, held at the Palais de Congres.

April: *Jardin'Art* (www.jardinsdumaroc.com/festival) is a celebration of Moroccan traditional and contemporary gardens.

June: *Marrakech Popular Arts Festival* (www.marrakechfestival.com) is a week-long bonanza of music, arts, folklore and a nightly fantasia (show on horseback) mainly located in the Badi Palace. Essaouira holds the *Gnaoua Festival of World Music* (www.festival-gnaoua.net), a world music event that attracts international performers and more than 200,000 music-lovers.

August: *The Moussem of Setti Fatma* celebrates the local saint after which the village in the Ourika was named.

September–October: *Marrakech Art Fair* (www.marrakechartfair.com/maf) exhibits contemporary art and is held in the grand Es Saadi hotel.

October: *MaRue'Kech* is a festival of theatre and street art, centred mainly around the Theatre Royal.

December: The *Marrakech International Film Festival* (www.enfestivalmarrakech.info) shows Moroccan and foreign films at cinemas around the city, attracting film stars and directors from around the globe.

EATING OUT

The best Moroccan food is found in the home, where the art of cooking and intricate recipes are passed down through the generations. The average Moroccan will rarely eat 'out' except perhaps at one of the simple restaurants or food stalls found in every town. Traditional Moroccan dishes take hours to prepare, so in restaurants, the food is often prepared a long time in advance and reheated. Remember that many specialities, such as couscous, *pastilla* or *mechoui* (slow roasted lamb), need to be ordered 24 hours in advance.

Restaurants

In Marrakech, as every-where else, the wise advice if you want to sample simple traditional food is to eat where local people eat. At the higher end of the price spectrum there are several wonderful places that reflect the rich range of Moroccan cooking itself, often producing modern twists on traditional dishes or creating huge feasts fit for a king – starting with a *pastilla* and ending, several courses later, with honey and nut encrusted *halwa* or exotically-spiced fruit. Several grand *riads* and palaces in the medina, like Dar Yacout,

Le Tanjia in the southern medina

Dar Zellij and Dar Moha (see page 108), offer such gourmet set menus in magnificently exotic surroundings – usually in open courtyards under the stars, with luxurious seating and sometimes classical Moroccan music. The food is good, albeit expensive by Moroccan (and even international) standards and most people can only do it once – the majority find it hard to get beyond the third course. Failing an invitation to a private home, order dinner in your *riad*: this will be the closest you get to home cooking.

Almost every week another restaurant opens its doors in Guéliz and Hivernage, with a new concept, an even trendier setting and a more 'fusioned' menu. Consistency is a problem, as the restless crowds of Marrakchis and expats move from new place to newer, and the chefs come and go. It is no secret that restaurant and *riad* owners often snatch staff from their competitors while out for dinner. In recent years the selection of restaurants in the new town has become very cosmopolitan with every cuisine represented from the popular Mediterranean dishes to Italian, Indian, Thai and increasingly sought-after Japanese sushi and sashimi.

Tagines, the traditional cookware

Meal Times

Breakfast is usually served around 8 or 9am and is either a French-style meal

of *café au lait* (milky coffee),
baguette and croissant, or
a delicious Moroccan-style
spread with flat Moroccan
bread *(khubz)*, *amlou* (paste
of crushed almonds with
honey and argan oil), *beghrir*
(a Moroccan pancake ver-
sion of crumpets) with jam
or honey, and freshly baked

rghaif (flat buttery layered pastry). All usually come with
freshly squeezed orange juice. **Lunch** is traditionally the
most important meal in the day, and is eaten at any time
between 1 and 4pm, when most shops (excluding the souks)
and offices are closed. Lunch usually means a selection of
salads and vegetable dishes, followed by a main course of
couscous, *tagine* or *mechoui* followed by a much needed
mint tea, sweets and most probably a little nap. If you are
in a hurry, there are plenty of faster options including *brochettes*, *merguez* (spiced sausages), sandwiches and quick-fix
tagines. **Dinner** is eaten after sunset, from 8 or 9pm onwards.
Most people eat a soup or lunch leftovers at home, but in
Marrakech families head to the 'Place', Jemaa el-Fna, for a
snack, while young people go out for a pizza or a bite with
drinks in Guéliz.

Local Specialities

Among the many culinary delights Marrakech has to offer,
don't leave without sampling the following regional favourites.

Bread

Bread, either the French baguette or Moroccan flat bread, is
eaten with every meal. It is always bought fresh from the local
hanout or corner shop just before the meal. Often it is used

instead of cutlery to scoop up vegetables or meat. Never take more bread than you need: Moroccans hold it in high regard as a 'gift from God', so it should never be wasted.

Couscous

Couscous is the national dish of Morocco, Algeria, Tunisia and Libya. The name comes from the Berber word *seksou*, and it consists of small grains of semolina.

In the West the fast-food pre-cooked version of couscous is most commonly found: you just need to add boiling water to the dry semolina and let it soak for a few minutes. In North Africa women traditionally make their own couscous by rolling two parts of semolina with one part of flour, some salted water and a little oil, until it is grain-sized. Once a batch is made it can be stored for a while. Couscous is steamed above a reduced broth of meat, vegetables and

Food stalls on the Jemaa el-Fna

spices, with which it is then served. It can be served with fish, as in Essaouira, or with just vegetables.

Diffa

The *diffa*, or Moroccan feast in someone's home or at a medina palace restaurant, consists of numerous courses. It starts with a selection of *mezze* or salads – between four and 10, mostly vegetables and dips eaten with bread, and *briouates*, tiny fried filo pastries stuffed with meat, cheese or spinach.

Ramadan

Most Moroccans don't eat or drink from sunrise to sunset during the Holy Month of Ramadan. They break the fast with the meal called *ftour*, have dinner later in the evening, and eat breakfast before the sun comes up. Many restaurants close for the month or only open for *ftour* with a special Ramadan menu, but in hotels and the more touristic areas of Marrakech many places remain open all day. Tourists are not expected to fast, but they should eat and drink out of public view.

The traditional Moroccan soup is *harira*, made with lamb broth, tomatoes, chickpeas and lots of spices. It is a hearty soup often served with a few dates on the side. (In Ramadan, the month of fasting, *harira* and dates are served at sundown to break the fast). Instead of soup – or after it – there is often *pastilla*, a delicious 'pie' with layers of *warka* (fine filo pastry) and pigeon or chicken cooked with caramelised onion and toasted almonds, then dusted with icing sugar and cinnamon. The lighter version of *pastilla* comes with seafood instead of meat. The main course is *couscous* with meat and/or the traditional *sept légumes* (seven vegetables), a choice of *tagines* (meat, chicken or fish stews, often cooked with some sort of fruit) or a *mechoui* (slow roasted lamb or goat). The traditional *mechoui*, a whole lamb or kid slow roasted in a clay oven, is often served for special occasions, like weddings. Fish is delicious in Morocco but is not often on the menu in Marrakech, except in the more western restaurants of the new town.

Dessert

Dessert in Morocco is often fresh fruit, particularly melon, watermelon or slices of orange sprinkled with cinnamon, spices and orange flower water. Sweet *pastilla au lait* consists of layers of *warka* filled with a light orange blossom-flavoured crème anglaise or custard and nuts. Mint tea is served with a selection of sweet pastries made with almonds, nuts or honey. The finest is the *Kaab el-ghzal* or *corne de gazelle* (gazelle's horn), a crusty pastry in a horn shape stuffed with almond paste perfumed with orange blossom. *Shebbakia* are fried pastries which are dipped in hot honey and sesame seeds, served during Ramadan.

Moroccan kebabs (*brochettes*) are typically lamb, chicken or beef

Traditional Dishes

bessara a thick soup of fava beans, olive oil and spices.

couscous perhaps Morocco's most famous dish. Of Berber origin, it is steamed semolina served with a broth of meat and vegetables – traditionally seven different ones.

harira rich lamb and chickpea soup eaten with dates.

loobia bean stew.

merguez hot spicy lamb sausages.

pastilla a multi-layered filo pastry with delicately sweetened pigeon.

ras el-hanout a mixture of 27 spices used on special occasions, particularly in stews.

tagine stew of meat or fish with fruit or vegetables, eaten with bread, cooked in the typical conical earthenware pot of the same name. One of the most traditional is *tgjine mqalli*: chicken with olives and preserved lemon. Another favourite is lamb with almonds and dates.

tanjia Festive Marrakchi dish of slow-cooked lamb stew in an urn-shaped earthenware crockpot, traditionally cooked for several hours in the embers of a *hammam* oven.

Cookery classes

Many *riad* hotels organise cookery classes where you can accompany the house chef to the local market and learn how to cook traditional Moroccan food such as *tagines*, *pastilla* or couscous. Some of the best classes are available from Souk Cuisine (tel: 0673-80 49 55; www.soukcuisine. com), which organises culinary weeks in Marrakech; La Maison Arabe (tel: 0524- 38 70 10; www.la maisonarabe.com); and Les Jardins de la Medina (tel: 0524-38 18 51; www.les jardinsdelamedina.com).

Drinks

Water and a variety of fizzy drinks are available everywhere, and are usually much cheaper than in Europe. In many places in Marrakech you can find delicious fresh juices; depending on the time of year they may include orange juice (plentiful on the Jemaa el-Fna), banana, avocado and carrot juice, and *lait d'amande* (almond milk). Make sure the juice is squeezed in front of you, and that the vendor doesn't add tap water.

Alcohol is forbidden by the Qur'an, so in theory Muslims do not drink it, although a lot of Marrakchis do. Many traditional Moroccan restaurants (mainly in the medina, but excluding *riad* restaurants) don't serve alcohol, but most of those (catering to tourists) in Guéliz and Hivernage do. The local beer is Flag, or the slightly more expensive, locally brewed Heineken and Casablanca, sold in beautiful bottles. In most tourist establishments foreign beers are also available. Since Roman times most of the local wines have been produced in Meknes, and plenty are very drinkable. The best reds are Volubilia, Médaillon, Domaine de Sahari, Guerrouane and Siroua. Good whites are Val d'Argan, Valpierre and

Spices flavour the cuisine

Cuvée President, while among the rosés the Sahari and Guerrouane are most recommended. The renowned French wine makers Châteauneuf du Pape are now producing a very good wine near Essaouira – the Val d'Argan red, rosé and white. For something typically Moroccan, *mahia* is a strong fig liqueur sometimes served as a *digestif*.

Mint tea

Moroccan coffee comes very strong and black; if you want it with milk ask for a *noss noss* or a *café au lait*. If you want milk with some coffee in it, ask for a *café cassé*. The most popular drink at any time of the day or night is *thé à la menthe*, or green tea with mint. Sometimes in winter the tea is served with *chiba* (absinthe) or *fliou* (menthol), and special guests are treated to mint tea with almonds or pine nuts.

Mint and Chinese Gunpowder Tea

Moroccan mint *(Mentha piperita)*, a fragrant kind of peppermint, is indigenous to Morocco. When in 1720 England's King George I offered the Sultan of Morocco a box of Chinese green tea as a gift, it was considered too pungent and bitter to drink neat, so the Moroccans mixed it with the sugar and mint widely available in the local markets. These days the tea is still made with Gunpowder tea, an inexpensive Chinese green tea which was originally rolled to preserve its freshness for the long journey from China to Africa. Mint tea has become the national drink of Morocco, and according to the Moroccan trade ministry, the country is the major importer of Chinese green tea worldwide.

TO HELP YOU ORDER...

Do you have a table?	**Avez-vous une table?**
I would like to book a table please	**Je voudrais réserver une table s'il vous plaît**
I'd like a/an/some...	**Je voudrais...**
The bill, please	**L'addition s'il vous plaît**
I'm a vegetarian	**Je suis végétarien, je ne mange pas la viande**
breakfast	**le petit déjeuner**
lunch	**le déjeuner**
dinner	**le dîner**
This is delicious	**C'est délicieux**

...AND READ THE MENU

fresh orange juice	**orange pressé**	lamb	**agneau**
(mineral) water	**de l'eau (minérale)**	chicken	**poulet**
		liver	**foie**
white coffee	**café au lait/ café crème/ noss noss**	fish	**poisson**
		prawns	**crevettes**
		squid	**calamar**
		vegetables	**légumes**
		fruit	**fruit**
mint tea	**thé à la menthe**	apple	**pomme**
		beans	**haricots**
black tea	**thé noir**	cactus fruit	**figue de Barbarie**
beer	**bière**	dates	**dates**
wine	**vin**	grapes	**raisins**
salt	**sel**	lemon	**citron**
pepper	**poivre**	pomegranate	**grenade**
garlic	**ail**	potatoes	**pommes de terre**
meat	**viande**		
brochettes	**kebabs**	pumpkin	**potiron**
beef	**boeuf**	watermelon	**pastèque**

PLACES TO EAT

The rates given here are for a three-course meal for one and include taxes and service, but not drinks.

€ under 100Dh   €€ 100–250Dh
€€€ 250–400Dh   €€€€ 400–600Dh
€€€€€ over 600Dh

JEMAA EL-FNA AND AROUND

Café Arabe €€–€€€ *184 rue el Mouassine, tel: 0524-42 97 28.* Daily 11.30am–11pm. This popular restaurant has seating both in a courtyard and on a stunning roof terrace with superb views over the medina. A great place to stop for lunch or for a romantic dinner. Mixture of Italian and Moroccan food.

Café des Epices €–€€ *75 Rahba Kedima, tel: 0524-39 17 70.* Daily 8am–8pm. No alcohol. A great place to hang out on the lively square of the Rahba Kedima. You can seek the shade inside or enjoy the views from the roof terrace, listen to cool music or chat with the young Moroccans who run the place. A perfect lunch spot with Wi-fi, mint tea, snacks, sandwiches and salads.

Café de France € *Jemaa el-Fna.* Daily 8am–11pm. No alcohol. This once famous café is not what it used to be, but still a good place for a mint tea away from the crowds, with great views over the city and Atlas Mountains from the rooftop.

Chez Chegrouni €–€€ *Jemaa el-Fna.* Daily 8am–11pm. No alcohol. Favourite old-timer in the square that still serves cheap but famously good, no-frills couscous, *tagines* and Moroccan salads.

Un Déjeuner à Marrakech €€ *2–4 place Douar Graoua, rue Riad Zitoun el Jedid, tel: 0524-37 83 97.* Daily 8am–8pm. No alcohol. A popular little café serving delicious food such as beef stroganoff, Caprese salad, vegetable tart, spinach and ricotta pie and *tarte au citron*. There is a little terrace with great views, too.

Le Marrakchi €€€ *52 rue des Banques, Jemaa el-Fna, tel: 0524-44 33 77, www.lemarrakchi.com.* Daily 11.30am–11pm. The Marrakchi has great views over the square, romantic decor on the second floor, and decent Moroccan food without too many spices. Unusually for restaurants on the square there is also a wine list. There is usually a belly-dancing show in the evenings.

Terrasses de l'Alhambra €€ *Jemaa el-Fna.* Daily 8am–11pm. No alcohol. A café-terrace, more elegant than most, serving a good espresso, ice cream and a menu of light snacks and salads. The terrace is a favourite meeting place, but on a hot day there is the attraction of air-conditioning inside.

Le Tobsil €€€€€ *22 Derb Abdellah ben Hessaien, Bab Ksour, tel: 0524-44 15 23.* Wed–Mon 7.30–11pm. One of the best medina palace restaurants – some say the best restaurant in Marrakech – serving an elaborate Moroccan set menu in spectacular surroundings with a good evening show of traditional music.

NORTHERN MEDINA

Dar Moha €€€€€ *81 rue Dar el Bacha, tel: 0524-38 64 00.* Tue–Sun lunch and dinner. The modern, inventive Moroccan cuisine served at Dar Moha is an amazing feast of flavours. Set around a romantic pool in a beautiful villa that once belonged to French fashion designer Pierre Balmain. Moha Fedal made his name and fame cooking traditional Moroccan dishes with a fusion twist. The food, part of a choice set menu, looks and tastes excellent, but the service can be hit and miss. Reservations essential.

Dar Yacout €€€€€ *79 rue Ahmed Soussi, tel: 0524-38 29 29.* Tue–Sun for dinner only. Dar Yacout is set in an opulently decorated palace, designed by Bill Willis. They serve a set menu, and it's quite a spectacle. Guests are led through the house, lit by 1,001 candles, before being served a true banquet. Book ahead and don't eat for days before you come.

Dar Zellij €€€€–€€€€€ *Kaasour, Sidi Ben Slimane, tel: 0524-38 26 27.* Daily, brunch and dinner. Dar Zellij is another stunning

17th century *riad*. Tables strewn with rose petals are arranged around a marble fountain. Feast on crispy *briouats*, fish *pastilla*, lamb *tagine* with figs or a Marrakchi *tanjia*. They also offer vegetarian and taster menus.

Le Foundouk €€€ *55 rue du Souk des Fassi, Kat Bennahid, tel: 0524-37 81 90, www.foundouk.com.* Tue–Sun noon–4pm and 7pm–midnight. Wildly stylish restaurant on several floors with a great roof terrace. Serves an attractive French-Moroccan menu.

Le Pavillion €€€€€ *47 Derb Zaouia, Bab Doukkala, tel: 0524-38 70 40.* Wed–Mon dinner only. Sit under the orange trees outside or in the small intimate salons inside for one of the more up-market eating experiences in Marrakech. The menu, mainly French with a few local flavours, is written on a blackboard, and the food, served in beautiful surroundings, is excellent.

Terrace des Epices €€ *15 Souk Cherifia, Sidi Abdelaziz, tel: 0524-37 59 04.* Daily 10am–midnight. Delightful venture from the team that owns the Café des Epices (see page 107), with a simple but gorgeous, vibrant terrace offering shaded booths, Wi-fi and cool lounge music. The menu is equally simple but delicious – keep some space for the prunes with fresh goat's cheese for dessert.

SOUTHERN MEDINA

Kosybar €€€ *47 place des Ferblantiers, tel: 0524-38 03 24.* Daily, 11am–1am. Kosybar is a popular meeting place for a sundowner or late-night drink and is located on the picturesque places des Ferblantiers near the Badi Palace. There is also good food available, ranging from Moroccan-Mediterranean dishes to Japanese prepared by the sushi chef. The owner is the son of a Moroccan vineyard owner, so the impressive wine list comes as no shock. At weekends there is live music in the piano bar.

Le Tanjia €€€€ *14 Derb Jdid, tel: 0524-38 38 36.* Daily, lunch and dinner. Oriental brasserie on the edge of the Jewish Mellah with sumptuous contemporary Moroccan decor, palm trees and elegant Moroccan cuisine. Waterpipes and tea on the terrace in the afternoon.

GUÉLIZ

Azar €€€ *corner of rue de Yougoslavie and boulevard Hassan II, tel: 0524-43 09 20.* Daily, lunch and dinner. Arguably the best Lebanese restaurant in Marrakech, Azar is set in glamorous, romantic surroundings. Mixing Moroccan and Lebanese food in a fun and modern way, Azar is usually always full with the chic crowd.

Bab Hotel €€€€ *corner of boulevard Mansour Eddahbi and rue Mohamed El Beqal, tel: 0524-43 52 50.* Daily, breakfast, lunch and dinner. The restaurant of the impossibly hip Bab Hotel serves up fantastic Mediterranean-western food. The super-cool, minimalist restaurant gets lively in the evenings and there is a great Ibiza-style terrace for both lunch and music in the evenings.

Café du Livre €–€€ *44 rue Tarik ibn Ziyad, tel: 0524-43 21 49.* Mon–Sat 9.30am–9pm. This café-cum-bookshop has an excellent selection on its shelves and the shop and the adjoining café-restaurant both have Wi-fi access. Excellent breakfast served until 11.30am. The lunch is Mediterranean-style and there is a selection of cakes in the afternoon.

Catanzaro €€ *42 rue Tarek ibn Ziyad, tel: 0524-43 37 31.* Mon–Sat lunch and dinner. This Italian-French restaurant becomes more popular by the year, and the quality is consistent. It can be relied on for excellent pizzas and grills and good desserts. There are now three sittings an evening and it is advisable to book ahead; as prices are good value it is popular with local families as well as tourists.

El-Fassia €€€€ *Résidence Tayeb, 55 boulevard Zerktouni, tel: 0524-38 38 39.* Daily for lunch and dinner. This famous Moroccan restaurant has been going for 20 years and is run by an all-women's cooperative. They serve a wider selection of classic Moroccan food than most, though the portions are typically huge. Specials like *mechoui* (roast lamb) need to be ordered 24 hours in advance. Reservations are essential.

Grand Café de la Poste €€€ *corner of boulevard Mansour ed-Dahbi and avenue Imam Malik, tel: 0524-43 30 38.* Daily 8am–1am. This is the place in town to see and be seen. The grand colonial-style terrace buzzes with *le tout Marrakech*, particularly at night. It's a great place for a drink, albeit an expensive one, and the simple fusion menu is good. A great one for people-watching.

Katsura €€ *rue Oum Errabia, tel: 0524-43 43 58.* Tue–Sun, lunch and dinner. One of the best Asian restaurants in town. The Thai chef whips up excellent Thai and Japanese dishes and the fantastic sushi and sashimi menu has everything from California to crispy king prawn rolls. The set menus for 100Dh are excellent value.

Kechmara €€€ *3 rue de la Liberté, tel: 0524-42 25 32, www.kechmara.ma.* Mon–Sat 7am–midnight. This is a popular laid-back restaurant, furnished in 1960s style, and serving a small menu of delicious light Mediterranean food. There's a great rooftop terrace for an alfresco lunch in spring and summer and revolving art exhibitions (all work for sale).

Libzar €€€€ *28 rue Moulay Ali, Tel: 0524-42 04 02.* Tue–Sun for lunch, daily for dinner. This isn't one of the best-known places but comments on the inventive Moroccan food, beautifully presented, and the romantic interior have been very positive. Owned and run by charming Assia Stitou.

Le Studio €€€ *87 avenue Moulay Rachid, tel: 0524-43 37 00.* Lunch Tue–Fri, dinner Mon–Sat. One of the best – and most affordable – French restaurants in town, Le Studio is wonderfully low-key, yet stylish. The excellent food includes mouthwatering steaks and various fresh fish dishes, as well as classics like snails, fois gras and *parmentier de canard*.

HIVERNAGE

Le Comptoir €€€€€ *avenue Ech-Chouhada, tel: 0524-43 77 02.* Daily 4pm–1am, until 2am at weekends. The food here is usually good, though can be unpredictable. People really come to this talked-about restaurant/bar/boutique/nightclub for the guaranteed party atmosphere, particularly when the belly dancers arrive every night at 10.30pm.

Crystal €€€€€ *Pacha Club, boulevard Mohammed VI, Zone Hôtelière, tel: 0524-38 84 80, www.pachamarrakech.com.* Daily for lunch and dinner. Within the Pacha nightclub compound, this elegant restaurant is run by the Michelin-starred Pourcel brothers. The menu is inventive Mediterranean with slight Italian overtones, using the best local produce mainly from the Ourika Valley. The restaurant has a pool so this makes a fun lunch option with a swim, and the atmosphere at the weekends is great.

Maï Thaï €€€€ *Villa la Saumuroise, corner of rue de Paris and avenue Echouhada, tel: 0524-45 73 01.* Tue–Sun, lunch and dinner. Considered the best Thai restaurant in town, Maï Thaï is situated in a beautiful Asian-style garden and the talented chefs produce a delicious blend of Asian and Thai cuisine using only the freshest ingredients. Takeaway and delivery also available.

La Table du Marché €€ *Hotel Hivernage, rue des Temples, tel: 0524-42 41 00.* Daily noon–midnight. Excellent brasserie, patisserie and tearoom that serves fine French tarts and croissants as well as delicious sandwiches. There is a pretty outside terrace as well.

AROUND MARRAKECH

Bô Zin €€€€€ *Km 5, Route de l'Ourika, tel: 0524-38 80 12.* Daily, dinner only. This hugely popular Asian restaurant just outside town is set in stunning bamboo gardens and has a wonderfully hip and romantic vibe. The food, though expensive, is famously good and the place gets lively later in the evenings, with a buzzing crowd and good music.

La Pause €€€€ *Douar Lmih Laroussième, Agafay, tel: 061-30 64 94, www.lapause-marrakech.com.* Daily for lunch and dinner. La Pause offers a Moroccan lunch or dinner with views of the desert, a relaxing time away from the buzz of Marrakech, and opportunity to camel ride, hike or see a spectacular sunset over the desert.

ESSAOUIRA

After 5 €€€ *7 rue Youssef El Fassi, tel: 0524-47 33 49*. Daily lunch and dinner. This beautiful restaurant, built into the walls of the medina with tables under traditional stone archways and ambient lighting, serves up the freshest and most delicious fish and seafood in Essaouira as well as excellent French bistro food.

Elizir €€€ *1 derb Agadir, tel: 0524-47 21 03.* Daily, dinner. Abdellatif must be the most charming restaurateur in the country. The setting is a traditional Moroccan townhouse but furnished with 1960s and 1970s pieces Abdellatif found in local junk markets. The Moroccan-Italian menu changes, but is always delicious and inventive, with dishes such as *tagines*, home-made ravioli with fresh goat's cheese, and steak with black chocolate sauce. The tapas that arrive at your table are on the house, as is mint tea. Reservations essential.

Ocean Vagabond €€ *boulevard Mohammed V, tel: 0524-78 39 34*. Daily, breakfast and lunch. This popular, breezy, laid-back café is nestled at the end of the beach (next to the Mistral Club). Day beds and deckchairs are screened from the wind and sand by bushy trees. The food is excellent – fresh fish, wood-fired pizzas, sandwiches – and the atmosphere suitably beachy.

Ristorante Silvestro €€€ *70 rue Laalouj, tel: 0524-47 35 55*. Daily, dinner. This well-kept secret is arguably the best Italian restaurant in Morocco and excellent value. Using imported ingredients from Italy and seasonal food and fish from Essaouira's markets, Giuseppe Silvestro and Rhounai Nezha produce mouthwatering pizzas and exquisite pastas and meat dishes. Cash only.

Taros €€€ *place Moulay Hassan, tel: 0524-47 64 07*, Mon–Sat 11am–4pm and 6pm–midnight. The Taros rooftop bar sits atop a tall house overlooking the harbour and main square. This is the place for a cocktail later in the evening, while the seagulls perform their aerial ballet. On the first floor there is a salon with a large library of books about Morocco, a boutique and a good restaurant serving very good Moroccan and French food, including many seafood dishes.

A–Z TRAVEL TIPS

A Summary of Practical Information

A

ACCOMMODATION

By law, prices must be displayed in reception and in the rooms. The quoted rates usually include VAT (TVA in French), but other local taxes – Taxe Promotion Touristique (TPT) and Taxe de Séjour (TS) – may add another 8–12Dh per night to your bill. Check also whether breakfast is included.

Do you have a single/double room?	**Avez-vous une chambre pour une personne/double?**
with bath/shower	**avec bain/douche**
with double bed/ twin beds	**avec un double lit/ deux lits**
What's the rate per night?	**C'est combien la nuit?**

AIRPORT

Marrakech's **Menara Airport (RAK)** tel: 0524-44 79 10, is 5km (3 miles) southwest of town. The arrivals hall has banks, exchange booths, ATMs and car rental agencies. A shuttle bus also runs between the airport and Hivernage, Guéliz, Jemaa el-Fna, Bab Doukkala and the train station, departing from the airport between 6am and 12.30am. A single ticket is 20Dh, a return, 30Dh. The easiest way to get into town is by *petit taxi* (meter taxi for a maximum of three passengers). They should charge around 30Dh for a journey into the centre of town but often charge more; they park outside the terminal. *Grands taxis* or shared taxis that will take up to six passengers charge around 100–150Dh to the Jemaa el-Fna or Guéliz – there are prices posted on the notice board, though these are largely ignored.

If it is the first time you have visited a particular *riad* or hotel in the medina or the Palmeraie, ask the hotel for a transfer, as the taxi driver may have trouble finding the place in the maze of the medina's alleys or the *pistes* in the Palmeraie. Prices for transfers are usually quite reasonable.

Where can I get a taxi?	**Où est-ce que je peux trouver un taxi?**
How much is it to the Jemaa el-Fna?	**Combien ça coute pour aller à la Jemaa el-Fna?**
Does this bus go to…?	**Est-ce que ce bus va jusqu' à …?**

B

BUDGETING FOR YOUR TRIP

Life in Morocco is cheaper than in most European countries, but prices in Marrakech tend to be higher than elsewhere in the country. During low season, it is always worth asking for a discounted rate for hotel rooms.

Accommodation. A double room in a *riad* in the medina starts at 500Dh (£37/$60), mid-range is about 1,200Dh (£90/$144) and quickly soars to over 2,500Dh (£189/$300), including all taxes and breakfast.

Bicycle and moped hire. Rates are negotiable, but average around 100Dh (£7.50/$12) a day. Motorbikes (125cc) cost from 200Dh (£14/$24) a day.

Entertainment. Nightclub admission (depending on the nightclub and sometimes including first drink), 200Dh.

Guides. Official guides, hired through the local tourist office, or contact the Moroccan National Tourist Office (tel: 0537-67 40 13, www.visitmorocco.com) charge from 120Dh per half-day.

Flights. A flight from London to Marrakech can cost anything from £100/$160 to £500/$800 depending on the season and the airline.

Local transport. City buses have a flat fare of 3Dh (0.23p/$0.38). Long-distance coach (CTM), one-way: Casablanca–Marrakech 80Dh (£6.25/$10.20); Marrakech–Ouarzazate 80Dh (£6.25/$10.20).

Taxis. Cross-town trip in a *petit taxi*: about 10–15Dh (0.78p/$1.30), depending on time of day (fares increase at night). A *grand taxi* is more – usually from 50Dh (£4/$6) in the day.

Meals. A three-course meal for two with Moroccan wine in a mid-range restaurant will cost about 600Dh; a coffee about 20Dh; and a beer 40–60Dh depending on the venue. You can eat in a good but basic grill restaurant for about 150Dh for two.

Sightseeing. The entrance fee to most sights is 10–15Dh (0.78p/$1.30).

C

CAMPING

There are two camping sites, but they are both a fair distance out of town. **Camping Caravaning Ferdaous** (11km/7 miles out of town on the Casablanca Road; tel: 0524-30 40 90/061-55 28 43) is beside the highway and therefore quite noisy, and there is no public transport, but it is shady and the facilities are clean. **Camping Le Relais de Marrakech** (10km/6 miles on the Marrakech Road; tel: 0664-71 73 28; www.lerelaisdemarrakech.com) has a swimming pool, as well as nomad tents and rooms and is clean.

CAR HIRE *(Voiture de location; see also Driving)*

You don't need a car to get around Marrakech; it is easier to walk or take a *petit taxi* for longer distances, but to see the surrounding area it is worth having your own transport. Most of the international car rental agencies, such as Hertz, Avis, Budget and Europcar, have offices at Marrakech airport and in town, but local agencies are often cheaper. Many companies offer discounts of up to 30 percent if you book in advance online, but do shop around, as prices vary quite a lot.

Car hire is relatively expensive and it pays to shop around. Prices for a compact car with manual transmission, mandatory liability insurance, unlimited mileage but without air-conditioning will cost from 600Dh (£45/$72) a day, but is slightly cheaper when you rent for a week. Hiring a *grand taxi* and driver for the day costs around 800Dh (£60/$96), depending on distance, often more if organised through your hotel. Fuel currently costs around 7Dh (£0.52/$0.84) per litre for diesel and 10Dh (£0.75/$1.20) for unleaded.

The minimum age for driving is 18, but most car rental companies require drivers to be at least 21. You must carry your driving licence, international or EU, and passport at all times.

Read your rental agreement carefully. Most contracts don't cover you for off-road driving, so you are not covered for damages or if you break down on *pistes*.

Avis: Marrakech Menara Airport, tel: 0524-43 31 69; www.avis.com.
Budget: Marrakech Menara Airport, tel: 0524-37 02 37; www.budget.com.
Europcar: 63 boulevard Zerktouni, tel: 0524-43 12 28; www.europcar.com.
Hertz: 154 boulevard Mohammed V, tel: 0524-44 99 84; www.hertz.co.uk.

I'd like to rent a car.	**J'aimerai louer une voiture.**
tomorrow	**demain**
for one day/week	**pour un jour/pour la semaine**
Is insurance included?	**Est-ce que l'assurance est inclue?**
unlimited mileage	**kilométrage illimité**

CLIMATE

Marrakech has mild winters and very hot summers. The best times to visit are in spring and autumn, when the temperatures are around 20 to 25°C (68–77°F), and around 10°C (50°F) at night. From November to March it may be sunny during the day but it gets cold at night, so make sure to book accommodation with heating. This is also the time for occasional rainfall. There is the chance of a desert storm in April, and a hot desert wind blows in June. In the summer it gets really hot, often in the high 30s or over 40°C (104°F). In summer many Marrakchis head for the coast or the mountains.

	J	F	M	A	M	J	J	A	S	O	N	D
°C	18	19	22	23	27	31	36	36	32	27	22	19
°F	64	66	72	73	81	88	97	97	90	81	72	66

CLOTHING (Vêtements)

You never really have to dress warmly in Marrakech; just bring a sweater or warm shawl for cold winter nights and appropriate clothing if you plan to head into the mountains or go trekking. In spring and autumn bring a warm fleece and a rain jacket, but most of the time light clothes will be fine. Summer is very hot, so stick to light cotton clothing, swimwear for the pool and a sun hat. During the day the dress code is very relaxed but at night people dress up to go out to the trendier restaurants and bars.

Many Moroccan women still wear a long kaftan and veil or headscarf when they go out, so if you don't want to stand out too much, and in order to respect local customs, women should avoid going to the souks or wandering around the medina in skimpy shorts or seethrough clothing. Men should refrain from removing their shirts in town, however hot it may be. Topless sunbathing is rarely permitted.

CRIME AND SAFETY (See also Emergencies and Police)

Marrakech is traditionally safer than most European cities, but visitors should still take the usual precautions. Women should make sure their handbags are closed, and slung across their shoulders, and everyone should carry valuables and wallets in inside pockets. Do not produce large sums of money when you are making a purchase. Watch out for pickpockets in crowded places, particularly the Jemaa el-Fna and the souks. Muggings are pretty rare. As so many people now stay in the medina, it has become safer to walk there at night, although some of the *riads* now pay for extra security near the entrances to the medina.

Morocco is the world's largest cannabis producer. Moderate local use is tolerated by the police, but the sale and consumption of drugs is strictly illegal.

If you are a victim of crime, call the police (or ask your hotel to do so for you) and contact your embassy or consulate (see page 121).

D

DRIVING (see also Car Hire)

You can drive in Marrakech, but traffic is becoming an issue. Most of the medina is pedestrianised so a car is not needed there. For most visitors a private taxi will be an easier way to navigate the city. Parking spaces are scarce, and the parking zones are watched by *gardiens de voitures* (parking attendants) in blue coats. They will more or less watch the car for you, and the going rate is about 10Dh for a few hours and 20–30Dh for overnight. In Guéliz there are a growing number of parking meters.

You only really need a car if you are going to explore the countryside. As you leave Marrakech there are Gendarmerie Royale checkpoints on the outskirts of town, and although foreigners are not usually stopped, it is advisable to slow down and say hello. Watch the signs for speed limits when driving out of the city as the likelihood of a policeman or a radar check is very high, and fines have to be paid on the spot. Always carry your passport and registration or car-rental documents with you.

Driving is on the right, overtaking on the left and seatbelts are compulsory. Speed limits are 120km/h (73mph) on toll roads, 100km/h (60mph) on highways, and 40 or 60km/h (25 or 38mph) in towns and cities. Traffic joining a road from the right has priority, unless signs or markings indicate otherwise. Cars already on a roundabout (traffic circle) must give way to those joining it. One local quirk you should be prepared for is that drivers making a left turn on a two-lane road often move over to the wrong side of the road before turning – this can be rather disconcerting if you are travelling in the opposite direction.

During the day the traffic can be chaotic but it is quite slow-moving. Avoid driving at night, if possible, as it can be dangerous.

Are we on the right road for...?	**Est-ce que nous sommes sur le bon chemin pour...**
Does this road lead to...?	**Est-ce que cette rue mène à...**
Fill the tank, please with... three star/four star diesel	**Le plein s'il-vous plaît, avec... normal/super gazole**
My car's broken down	**Ma voiture est en panne**
I have a flat tyre	**J'ai un pneu crevé**

E

ELECTRICITY

Morocco operates on 220V AC/50Hz. Plugs are of the European two-pin variety. Visitors from the UK and US will need a transformer to use their own appliances.

I need an adaptor/ battery, please.	**J'ai besoin d'un adapteur/d'une pile électrique s'il vous plaît.**

EMBASSIES AND CONSULATES

In Morocco

Most embassies and consulates are in Rabat. In Marrakech the Honorary British Consulate is currently closed until further notice, so contact should be made to the embassy in Rabat. Australia does not have a consulate or embassy in Morocco. Consular assistance is provided by the Canadian Embassy.

Canadian Embassy: 13 bis rue Jaafa as-Sadiq, Rabat; tel: 0537-68 74 00; www.rabat.gc.ca.

South African Embassy: 34 rue des Saadiens, Rabat; tel: 0537-70 67 60.

UK Embassy: 28 Avenue S.A.R. Sidi Mohammed Souissi, 10105 (BP 45) Rabat, tel: 0537-63 33 33, www.ukinmorocco.fco.gov.uk.

US Embassy: 2 avenue Mohammed el-Fassi, Rabat; tel: 0537-76 22 65; http://morocco.usembassy.gov. Consulate 8 boulevard Moulay Youssef, Casablanca, tel: 0522-26 45 50

Moroccan Diplomatic Missions Abroad

Australia: There is no Moroccan consulate or embassy in Australia. Consular assistance to Australian citizens in Morocco is provided by the Moroccan Consulate in Paris, 5, rue le Tasse, Paris; tel: (+33-1) 45206935.

Canada: Moroccan Embassy, 38 Range Road, Ottawa, Ontario K1N 8J4; tel: 613-236 7391/92; www.ambassade-maroc.ottawa.on.ca.

South Africa: Moroccan Embassy, 799 Schoeman Street, Arcadia, Pretoria 0083; tel: 012-343 0230.

UK: Moroccan Embassy, 49 Queen's Gate Garden, London SW7 5NE; tel: 020-7581 5001/4.

US: Consulate General of Morocco, 10 East 40th Street, New York, NY 10016; tel: 212-758 2625; www.moroccanconsulate.com.

Moroccan Embassy, 1601 21st Street, NW, Washington DC 20009; tel: 202-462 7979.

EMERGENCIES

The following numbers are useful 24 hours a day in an emergency:

Police 19

Fire 15

Brigade Touristique tel: 0524-38 46 01 (Tourist Police)

Ambulance tel: 0524-44 37 24

Polyclinique du Sud tel: 0524-44 79 99/76 19, 24-hour emergency care (2 rue de Yougoslavie – corner of rue de Yougoslavie and rue Ibn Aïcha, Guéliz).

G

GAY AND LESBIAN TRAVELLERS

Gay sex is illegal under Moroccan law; the Moroccan penal code prohibits any sex act with a person of the same sex and allows for imprisonment of six months to three years plus a fine. In reality, however, due to sexual segregation in the Muslim culture, homosexuality is relatively widespread. The concept of lesbianism is totally taboo in Morocco. That said, Marrakech is still a popular destination among British, American and French gay men and has clubs and bars that are openly gay.

GETTING THERE (see also Airport)

By air. Marrakech's airport is linked by daily scheduled direct flights to most European cities. An increasing number of budget carriers now fly to Marrakech. **Royal Air Maroc** operates a daily flight to Marrakech from London Heathrow via Casablanca. Sometimes this involves a long delay in Casablanca while waiting for connecting flights from other countries in Europe. Royal Air Maroc in the UK: Langham House, 32–33 Gosfield Street, London W1; tel: 020-7307 5800; www.royalairmaroc.com. In Marrakech: 197 avenue Mohammed V; tel: 0524-42 55 01; www.royalairmaroc.com.

Marrakech is well served by the following budget airlines: Easyjet (www.easyjet.com) flies from Gatwick to Marrakech. Ryanair (www.ryanair.com) flies from London Luton to Marrakech. Thomsonfly (www.thomsonfly.com) flies from Manchester, London Luton and Gatwick to Marrakech.

British Airways (www.ba.com) has started a route from London Heathrow to Marrakech and British Midland International (www.bmi.com) also flies from Gatwick to Casablanca and Marrakech.

By rail. It is possible to travel to Marrakech by train via Paris (Eurostar to Gare du Nord and then change to Gare d'Austerlitz) for Algeciras, where ferries leave for Tangier throughout the day. From Tangier there are three daytime trains to Marrakech (journey time 9–10 hours), but you're best off booking a couchette on the overnight train, which leaves daily at 9.05pm and arrives at 8.05am.

In Tangier you will need to take a taxi from the ferry terminal to the railway station as they are at opposite ends of the bay. The first-class couchettes accommodate four passengers in each compartment, and although not luxurious, are comfortable enough. There is normally only one couchette carriage so it is advisable to book your place in advance. Check out schedules and fares on www.oncf.ma. After taking the ferry from Algeciras to Tangier, it is a 600km (370-mile) drive along the new toll motorway to Marrakech.

By bus. The bus station (*gare routière*) is at Bab Doukkala.

By car. A good highway connects Marrakech with Casablanca. There is a new toll motorway to Essaouira and slower roads to Taroudant via the Tizi-n-Test, to Ouazarzate via the Tizi-n-Tichka and to Fez.

GUIDES AND TOURS

Marrakech Tour Bus (tel: 0525-06 00 06) is an open-top double decker bus with a running commentary in several languages, which follows two circular routes. Buses leave from place Abdelmoumen Ben Ali, opposite the Tourist Office, every 30 minutes for the first route from 9am–5pm and every 80 minutes from 9.50am–3.50pm for the second, but you can hop on or off where you like. The first route covers the sights in the city, the second does the Circuit de la Palmeraie. Tickets can be bought on board (130Dh) and are valid for 24 hours.

Guides. It is easy enough to find your way around the medina with a map or guidebook, but a good guide will provide more insight. An official guide can be obtained through your hotel or the Office National Marocain de Tourisme (ONMT; *see Tourist Information, page 132*).

H

HEALTH AND MEDICAL CARE

Morocco has good doctors *(médecins)* and most pharmacies have a decent supply of drugs, but it can be hard to find someone who speaks English. Ask your hotel concierge for a doctor, or contact the **Polyclinique du Sud** (corner of rue Ibn Aïcha and rue de Yougoslavie, Guéliz; tel: 0524-44 79 99) which has a 24-hour emergency medical and dental service, or **S.O.S Médecins** (tel: 0524-40 40 40) for an emergency call-out service (400Dh per consultation).

Most pharmacies (signified by a large green cross outside) are open Monday–Friday from 9am–noon and 3–7pm. Each pharmacy has a notice in the window giving the address of the *pharmacie de garde* – the pharmacy on duty until midnight or at weekends. The Polyclinique du Sud can provide emergency drugs after midnight.

The most common visitor ailments are upset stomachs and sunstroke. Don't drink tap water and avoid street food if you have a sensitive stomach; it's also wise to avoid undercooked meat, salads, fruit (unless you peel it yourself) and dairy products. Bring rehydration salts such as Dioralyte, wear a sunhat and drink plenty of bottled water.

Ensure you have travel insurance as Morocco has no reciprocal agreement with other countries to provide free medical care for visitors.

Where's the nearest (all night) pharmacy?	**Où est la pharmacie (de nuit) la plus proche?**
I need a doctor/ dentist	**J'ai besoin d'un médecin/ un dentiste**
an ambulance	**une ambulance**
hospital	**un hôpital**
I have an upset stomach	**J'ai mal au ventre**
sunburn/a fever	**un coup de soleil/une fièvre**

No immunisations are compulsory, but inoculations for tetanus, polio, typhoid and hepatitis A are recommended if travelling to rural areas.

L

LANGUAGE

Most people in Marrakech speak French and Moroccan Arabic, which differs from the Classical Arabic spoken in the Middle East. Quite a large number also speak Tashelhait or Chleuh, the local Berber language, and more and more people speak English. Below are some useful phrases to help you get by in French.

Do you speak English?	Est-ce que vous parlez anglais?
excuse me	pardon
you are welcome	je vous en prie
yes/no	oui/non
please	s'il vous plaît (formal), s'il te plaît
thank you	merci
where/when/how	Où/quand/comment
day/week/month/year	jour/semaine/mois/année
left/right	gauche/droite
near/far	près/loin
cheap/expensive	bon marché/cher
open/closed	ouvert/fermé
hot/cold	chaud/froid
old/new	vieux/nouveau
Please write it down	Est-ce que vous pouvez l'écrire?
What does it mean?	Qu'est-ce que cela veut dire?
Help me please	Aidez-moi s'il vous plaît
Just a minute	un moment
What time is it?	Il est quelle heure?

M

MEDIA (*média*)

The main European newspapers and the *International Herald Tribune* as well as many magazines are easily available in Marrakech, usually 24 hours old. The best newsstands are on avenue Mohammed V in Guéliz, on the corner of rue de Mauritanie and next door to the tourist office. Most local magazines are in French or Arabic. For listings, check the monthly French-language free sheet *Couleurs Marrakech Pocket* (www.marrakechpocket.com), available from more up-market restaurants and shops and also the *Tribune de Marrakech*, also available free from most hotels and restaurants.

MONEY (*Argent*)

The local currency is the Moroccan dirham, abbreviated Dh or mad. The dirham is divided into 100 centimes or francs. Coins of 5, 10, 20 and 50 centimes and of 1, 5 and 10 dirhams are in circulation, along with notes of 20, 50, 100 and 500 dirhams.

Everyone is always short of change, particularly taxi drivers, so hang on to yours if you can; it makes transactions easier.

Currency exchange. The easiest currency to carry is euros, but British pounds sterling and US dollars are easily exchangeable at Moroccan banks.

Bureaux de change near the Jemaa el-Fna are open longer hours, and the Hotel Ali (rue Moulay Ismail) as well as other main hotels will exchange money at any time at a less favourable rate. Keep your receipt, as you can exchange excess dirhams into your own currency at the airport.

Credit cards, travellers cheques and ATMs. International credit cards are widely accepted, although some smaller shops and restaurants will only accept cash. Travellers cheques are accepted by most banks but stick to the better-known brands such as American Express and Thomas Cook. A commission is usually charged.

There are numerous cashpoints (atms, *distributeur automatique*) all over Marrakech and Essaouira, but it is harder to find one out in the countryside. The exchange rate is better than for cash or travellers cheques, but your bank will probably charge you for the withdrawal. The withdrawal limit per day is 5,000Dh, but this depends on the bank. If you need more, take your card and passport to an exchange office or bank and take out a cash advance.

Can I pay with this credit card?	**Je peux payer avec une carte?**
I want to change some pounds/dollars	**Je veux changer des livres anglais/dollars**
Can you cash a travellers' cheque?	**Vous changez des chèques de voyage?**
Where is the bank/ currency exchange/ cash machine?	**Où se trouve la banque/ le bureau de change/ distributeur automatique?**
How much is it?	**C'est combien?**

O

OPENING TIMES

The working week is generally from Monday–Friday with a half day on Saturday, but some shops in the medina are open daily, while some close on Friday afternoon.

Banks. Winter: Mon–Fri 8.30am–11.30am and 2.30–4pm; summer: Mon–Fri 8.30–11.30am and 3–5pm; Ramadan: Mon–Fri 9.30am–3pm.

Shops. Mon–Sat 9am–12.30pm, 2.30–8pm. Some shops close on Friday (the Muslim holy day) or even Saturday if the owner is Jewish. In the new parts of cities shops often close on Sunday. Other shops remain open throughout the week. Generally, western shops in the

Ville Nouvelle will keep similar opening hours to those in Europe, opening a bit later in the morning but without closing for lunch.

Museums and sights. Generally 9am–noon and 3–6pm; most close on Tues. Most religious buildings, such as madrassas, will close for a period, or all day, on Friday.

Offices: Mon–Thurs 8.30am–noon, 2.30–6pm, Fri: 8.30am–noon, 3–6.30pm, Ramadan: 9.30am–3 or 4pm. Government offices close early on Friday and many private businesses open on Saturday morning.

P

POLICE (See also Crime and Safety, and Emergencies)

The main police station (Hôtel de Police) is on rue Oued el-Makhazine in Guéliz near Jnane Harti (emergency tel: 19), but any crime against a tourist should immediately be reported to the Brigade Touristique (Tourist Police), on the northern side of the Jemaa el-Fna (tel: 0524-38 46 01). The Gendarmerie Nationale is in control of the roads, and they frequently set up posts just outside the city to catch those speeding. Fines need to be paid on the spot.

Where's the nearest police station?	**Où est le bureau de police le plus proche?**
I've lost my wallet/ bag/passport	**J'ai perdu ma portefeuille/ mon sac/mon passeport**

POST OFFICE (Bureau de poste)

The main post office (PTT Centrale) is on place du 16 Novembre in Guéliz. It's open Monday–Saturday 8.30am–6.30pm and is usually closed at lunchtime. There is a branch on rue Moulay Ismail near the Jemaa el-Fna (Monday–Friday 8am–3pm). Stamps can also be bought at hotel reception desks or at a *tabac* (cigarettes stall). The mail service is very slow, so if your mail is urgent, use the express service (EMS) or an international courier service.

Where's the post office?	**Où est la poste?**
express (special delivery)	**expresse**
a stamp	**une timbre**
air mail	**par avion**

PUBLIC HOLIDAYS (Jours Fériés)

There are two kinds of holiday in Morocco: secular and religious. Banks, post offices, government offices and many other businesses will be closed on the following secular holidays:

Jan 1	New Year's Day
Jan 11	Independence Manifesto Day
May 1	Labour Day
July 30	Feast of the Throne
Aug 14	Reunification Day
Aug 20	People's Revolution Day
Aug 21	King Mohammed VI's Birthday and Young People's Day
Nov 6	Anniversary of the Green March
Nov 18	Independence Day

Religious holidays. Muslim festivals follow the lunar Hegira calendar, a few days shorter than the Western solar calendar. *Fatih Muharram* is the Muslim New Year. Ten days later, the *Achoura* commemorates the assassination of Hussein, grandson of Mohammed. The *Aïd es-Seghir*, or *Aïd el Fitr*, marks the end of Ramadan and most offices and shops are closed for two days. The *Aïd el-Kebir*, 70 days later, is a two-day holiday during which families slaughter a lamb to commemorate Abraham's willingness to sacrifice his son. *Aïd el-Mouloud* is the birthday of the Prophet Mohammed.

R

RELIGION

Morocco is a Muslim country, but is tolerant of other religions. Christians account for about 1 percent of the population. Most Moroccans belong to the Sunni branch of Islam. Muslims pray five times a day in the direction of Mecca (Saudi Arabia), and go to the mosque particularly for the Friday midday prayer. Most mosques and religious buildings are closed to non-Muslims. Muslims fast between the hours of sunrise and sunset during the holy month of Ramadan, and during this month visitors should eat and drink discreetly during the day.

The tourist office can provide a list of religious services for English-speaking Roman Catholic visitors, but there is no Anglican church in the city. Access to mosques and holy places in Marrakech is restricted to Muslims, with the following exceptions: Madrassa Ben Youssef (see page 40) and the mosque in Tin-Mal (see page 73).

T

TELEPHONES

Morocco's international code is 212, the code for Marrakech is 0524, and this area code needs to be dialled even within the region. To call abroad from Morocco dial first 00 then the country code (44 for UK, 1 for the US), followed by the phone number.

Telephone calls can be made from phone boxes *(cabines)* on the street or in a main post office. They take Dh1 and Dh5 coins or phone cards; the latter are available from *tabacs*, news vendors or phone shops. It is best to use a phone card for international calls. Private pay-phone booths *(téléboutiques)* are widespread; clean and efficient, they cost little more than a pay phone on the street. Most mobile phones work in Morocco and roaming is available but predictably expensive.

TIME ZONES

Morocco follows Greenwich Mean Time (GMT) all year round. It is on the same time as Britain in winter, but an hour behind during British Summer Time.

TIPPING

In cafés and restaurants a tip (*pourboire*) of 10–15 percent of the total bill should be given. Everybody else who peforms a service for you will expect a small tip of 10–20Dh. This includes attendants (*gardiens*) at monuments and museums as well as porters and parking attendants.

TOILETS

There are very few public toilets in Morocco, so always use the facilities in a hotel or restaurant if possible. Carry some toilet paper as it is not always available.

Where are the toilets?   **Où sont les toilettes?**

TOURIST INFORMATION

The main tourist office in Marrakech is on place Abdelmoumen, Guéliz (tel: 0524-43 61 31). The office is open Mon–Fri 8.30am–4.30pm, and Saturday morning. The Moroccan Tourist Offices (ONMT; Office National Marocain de Tourisme; www.visitmorocco.com) has good information on Marrakech and the rest of the country.

TRANSPORT

Local buses. There are few local buses in Marrakech. Most of those that do exist operate between the city centre and the suburbs to take local people between home and work, and are not really useful to visitors. Bus number 1 leaves from the place de Foucault near the Jemaa el-Fna and goes to Guéliz along the avenue Mohammed V. Buses 3 and 8 run from the same square to the train station on avenue Hassan II.

Taxis. The best way of getting around town is by taxi, although these do not exactly constitute public transport. The *petit taxi* can take a maximum of three passengers, cannot leave city limits and charges by the meter so make sure it is switched on. Expect to pay 50 percent more from 8pm onwards. A taxi from the Jemaa el-Fna to Guéliz costs about 10Dh. The *grands taxi* is inexpensive and takes up to six passengers. There are no fixed departure times; the taxi departs when all the seats are full. You simply turn up at the 'terminal' (the tourist office or your hotel will tell you where this is; it is often next to the main bus station).

Intercity buses. The bus station (*gare routière*) is at Bab Doukkala, outside the medina walls. There are long-distance buses to most Moroccan cities operated by ctm (www.ctm.ma) or the superior Supratours (run by the train company, ONCF www.oncf.ma), who run the fastest bus to Essaouira (roughly 3.5 hours). Except on these express services, which have air-conditioning and videos, bus travel over long distances can be uncomfortable. If you have a choice, it is better to take the train.

Trains. Trains are operated by the national railway company ONCF (www.oncf.ma). The railway station is on avenue Mohammed VI. As

Where can I get a taxi?	**Où est-ce que je peux trouver un taxi?**
What's the fare to ... ?	**C'est combien pour le billet de...?**
Where is the bus stop?	**Où est l'arrêt de bus?**
When's the next bus to ...?	**Le prochain bus pour.... part quand?**
A ticket to ...	**Un billet pour...**
single/return	**Aller/aller retour**
Will you tell me when to get off?	**Est-ce que vous pourriez me dire où je dois descendre?**

the southernmost terminal, Marrakech has regular connections with Casablanca, Rabat, Tangier, Oujda, Fez and Meknes.

Buses go from the station to the Jemaa el-Fna, and a line of *petits taxis* wait outside the station – a journey should cost from 10–20Dh. There are no trains further south or to Essaouira.

VISAS AND ENTRY REQUIREMENTS

A current passport is required for entry to Morocco, and it must be valid for at least six months after the date of entry. Visas are not required for visits lasting under three months for EU, US, Canadian, Australian and New Zealand citizens, but South Africans must apply for a visa at the Moroccan embassy in Pretoria. When you arrive you will be given an official form to fill in, stating profession, address(es) in Morocco and length of stay.

Currency restrictions. Visitors can carry unlimited amounts of foreign currency in and out of the country, but all amounts exceeding 15,000Dh in foreign currency must be declared. It is illegal to import or export Moroccan Dirhams.

Customs. Visitors can bring in 1 litre of liquor, 1 litre of wine, 200 cigarettes or 50 cigars, and 5g of perfume duty-free.

WEBSITES

The most useful websites are:

www.morocco.com Includes hotel booking and travel tips.
www.hipmarrakech.com Good list of *riads* and restaurant guide.
www.ilovemarrakech.com Online travel guide.
www.bestrestaurantsmaroc.com Restaurant listings.
www.morocco-holidays-guide.co.uk Listings (sites, hotels) for the major cities.

Recommended Hotels

Fifteen years ago, most of the hotels in Marrakech were uninspiring and situated in Guéliz. Today, there is a fantastic assortment of places that cater to every taste and budget. From charming guesthouses and rural retreats to boutique *riads*, luxury resorts and large international hotels, there is something to suit everyone. But it is the city's romantic, exotic *riads* in the medina (800 at the last count) that draw the most tourists and are arguably the most atmospheric and memorable places to stay.

Riads are not traditional hotels: they rarely have a minibar, TV or room service and cannot be easily categorised, but they offer an experience that is hard to beat and a level of attention to detail and personal service not usually found elsewhere. Most *riads* can be rented in their entirety, provide invaluable local advice on Marrakech and will organise day trips and guided tours. Outside Marrakech there is a scattering of tranquil country escapes, and in the famed Palmeraie there are some of the most exclusive boutique hotels. Websites such as www.hipmarrakech.com, www.ilovemarrakech.com and www.boutiquesouk.com are good resources for finding *riads*.

It is essential to book in advance over the peak seasons of Christmas, New Year and Easter and it is always worth looking out for deals and packages during the low seasons.

Prices given here are for a standard double room in high season, including breakfast.

€€€€€	over €350
€€€€	€250–350
€€€	€100–250
€€	€70–100
€	under €70

JEMAA EL-FNA AND AROUND

Dar Attajmil €€€ *23 rue Laksour, off rue Sidi el-Yamami, tel: 0524-42 69 66, www.darattajmil.com.* Right in the middle of the chic El

Ksour area, this four-room *riad* is a little oasis. Very welcoming and stylishly decorated with Italian good taste. The rooms overlook a courtyard with banana trees and palms, and the roof terrace is bliss. There are also cookery courses, which include a visit to the local food market.

Dar Eliane €€ *39 Derb Maada, tel: 0524-37 57 10, www.dareliane. com*. In the heart of the souks, Dar Eliane offers all the charm and exoticism of a Moroccan *riad*, but without the price tag so often associated with good quality places. There is a lovely whitewashed courtyard, four pretty ensuite rooms, a traditional Moroccan kitchen and salon with fireplace, and a large roof terrace complete with Berber tent and barbecue. Lunch and dinner (all food is organic) on request and the *riad* can be rented in its entirety.

Hotel Sherazade € *3 Derb Jemaa, tel: 0524-42 93 05, www.hotelsherazade.com*. Once the house of wealthy merchants, Hotel Sherazade is fantastically located, just south of Jemaa el-Fna, and is excellent value for somewhere so close to the main square. The *riad* is spotlessly clean and run by helpful multi-lingual staff; most rooms have ensuite bathrooms, those on the terrace have shared facilities. Day trips to the Atlas, Ourika Valley and the Atlantic coast can be arranged on request.

Jnane Mogador € *116 Riad Zitoun el-Kedim, tel: 0524-42 63 23, www.jnanemogador.com*. This small charming *riad* with 17 clean, comfortable rooms offers very good value for money and therefore fills up quickly, so book ahead. The terrace gives fabulous views of the medina and the Atlas Mountains. No heating in winter.

La Mamounia €€€€€ *avenue Bab Jdid, tel: 0524-38 86 00, www. mamounia.com*. La Mamounia is the most iconic hotel in town, where everyone from Winston Churchill to the Rolling Stones has stayed. Having undergone a lavish restoration, she is back and better than ever. All rooms have a view of the magnificent gardens and Atlas Mountains. There are three elegant restaurants – Le Marocain, L'Italien and Le Français – as well as the legendary Churchill Bar, an award-winning wellness spa and casino.

Riad el-Fenn €€€€ *Derb Moulay Abdallah ben Hezzian, Bab el-Ksour, tel: 0524-44 12 10, www.riadelfenn.com.* Three houses have been brought together, and everything is light, spacious, uncluttered and tranquil at this *riad* belonging to Vanessa Branson (sister of Richard). There are three pools, including one on the roof, a bar with a mirrored ceiling, a spa, library, movie room and organic garden.

Riad de l'Orientale €–€€ *8 Derb Ahmar, Quartier Laksour, tel: 0524-42 66 42, www.riadorientale.com.* Small family-run *riad* in a 250-year old house with comfortable rooms. A far cry from designer boutique hotels, the British owners have kept the traditional Moroccan style and offer a warm welcome. Wi-fi access throughout.

Riad W €€–€€€ *41 Derb Boutouil, tel: 0665-36 79 36, www.riadw. com.* Minutes from Jemaa el-Fna is one of the most stylish *riads* in the medina. Riad W is the height of simplicity with a fashionable and modern feel with stripped-back wooden doors and exposed brickwork. The rooms are cosy, there is a little plunge pool in the courtyard and the roof terrace is a lovely place to unwind and have breakfast or lunch.

NORTHERN MEDINA

Dar Soukaina €€ *19 Derb al Ferrane, Riad Laarouss, tel: 0661-24 52 38, www.darsoukaina.net.* This is a peaceful *riad* decorated with subtlety – whitewashed walls, simple fabrics and gentle colours. Two courtyards are shaded by a huge orange tree and banana plants, and there is a secluded roof terrace with a cushion-filled Berber tent.

Dar Tchaikana €€–€€€ *25 Derb el-Ferrane, Riad Laarous, tel: 0524-38 51 50, www.tchaikana.com.* With subtle white and light interiors softened by beautiful sub-Saharan textiles, this is a chic and laid-back hotel with just four large rooms around a splendid courtyard. The place is run smoothly by a welcoming young Belgian couple who love to share their knowledge of Marrakech with their clients.

Dar Vedra €€–€€€ *3 Derb Sidi Ahmed Ou Moussa, tel: 0524-38 93 70, www.darvedra.com.* A faithfully restored 18th-century *riad*, Dar Vedra has seven beautifully designed bedrooms and one large suite, a sitting room with open fire, a pretty plunge pool outside that is heated in winter and a fabulous roof terrace. The views across the medina are some of the best.

Maison Arabe €€€€ *1 Derb Assehbe, Bab Doukkala, tel: 0524-38 70 10, www.lamaisonarabe.com.* La Maison Arabe began its life as a famous restaurant in 1946 and has become one of Marrakech's most well-known hotels. There are antiques everywhere, lots of cosy places to sit, elegant rooms, two pools (one in a country club outside town), three restaurants and a spa. It is also famous for its cookery school.

Riad 72 €€€–€€€€ *72 Arset Aouzal, tel: 0524-38 76 29, www.riad72.com.* In the heart of the prestigious Dar el Bacha quarter, this hip *riad* evokes all the splendour of traditional Moroccan design, but with modern twists. The four suites are super romantic, there is a bookshop, a spa with *hammam* and the services of a yoga teacher and masseuse. The roof terrace with plunge pool has exceptional views.

Riad Charai €€€€ *54 Diour Jdad, tel: 0524-43 72 11, www.riadcharai.com.* Riad Charai was once the residence of the Private Secretary to Glaoui, Pasha of Marrakech. There is a wonderful pool and the garden, where meals are eaten, is shaded with orange trees and cooled by a fountain. There are eight luxurious suites, a spa and *hammam* and the *riad* can be rented in its entirety.

Riad Farnatchi €€€€€ *2 Derb el-Farnatchi, Qa'at Benahid, tel: 0524-38 49 10, www.riadfarnatchi.com.* Five houses in the heart of the medina have been transformed into a sumptuous and intimate hotel, with nine luxurious suites, a *hammam*, pool and spa and a manager who knows all the ins and outs of Marrakech.

Riad Tarabel €€€€ *8 Derb Sraghna, Dar el-Bacha, tel: 0524-39 17 06, www.riadtarabel.com.* Riad Tarabel is one of the most beautifully restored *riads* in the medina and quietly unique in its design. With chic grey woodwork, an unusual grassy courtyard shaded by orange trees, three elegant rooms, a roof terrace and *hammam*, this is the ultimate place to get away from it all, whilst still being at the centre of things.

Tlaatawa Sitteen €–€€ *63 Derb el-Ferrane, Riad Laarous, tel: 0524-38 30 26, www.tlaatawasitteen.com.* Offers excellent value and neat, simple and comfortable rooms. Proprietors Kamaal, his brother Saeed and Najjat welcome their guests like long-lost friends, and every night somehow turns into a gathering. This is old-style Marrakech, and Najjat's cooking is strongly recommended.

SOUTHERN MEDINA

Angsana Riads €€€€€ *rue Riad Zitoun el-Jdid, tel: 0524-388 905, www.angsana.com.* The Angsana-Banyan Tree is the first international hotel chain to move into the medina. They run six beautiful *riads* just off rue Riad Zitoun el-Jdid in the southern medina (same contact details for all of them). All have spas, for which the company is famous, and each has its own individual atmosphere and decor. The restaurants serve Asian fusion cuisine.

Dar el Souk €–€€€ *56 Derb Jdid, tel: 0524-39 15 68, www.darelsouk. com.* Dar el Souk is located just off the popular shopping street of rue Riad Zitoun el Kedim and minutes from the sights and palaces of the southern medina. This vibrant *riad* is bursting with flowers and has twin roof terraces covered in cushions overlooking the whole of Marrakech. Rooms are individually decorated and have private outside seating areas.

Riad Kaiss €€€€€ *65 Derb Jedid, off Riad Zitoun el-Kedim, tel: 0524-44 01 41, www.riadkaiss.com.* Another stunning *riad* renovated and owned by French architect Christian Ferré, who kept the Moroccan style of the house while adding a contemporary architectural touch. The result is eye-catching and calming, with beautiful earth-coloured spaces and a cool dip pool.

Riad Kasbah €€€ *101 Derb Harbil, Kasbah; tel: 0524-45 88 00.* Perfectly located near the Saadian Tombs, this small guesthouse, with

10 rooms and suites around a dip pool and large courtyard, is decorated in muted colours but also has many touches of the warm reds and yellows of Marrakech. Guests can use the private traditional indoor *hammam*.

La Sultana €€€€€ *rue de la Kasbah, Kasbah, tel: 0524-38 80 88, www. lasultanamarrakech.com.* Next to the Badi, Bahia and Royal Palaces, this palace *riad* evokes the grandeur of Imperial Marrakech in a historic setting. There are 28 suites, as well as private living rooms and hanging gardens. The courtyard pool shares a wall with the Saadian Tombs and there is a Jacuzzi on the huge roof terrace, which has views of the Atlas.

Hotel du Trésor € *77 Sidi Boulokat, off Riad Zitoun el-Kedim, tel: 0524-37 51 13, www.hotel-du-tresor.com.* Totally delightful little hotel, opened in the 1950s, and now owned by an Italian, who kept the traditional courtyard and tiles but added some funky objects, mostly from other historic hotels in the town. The rooms are set around a quiet courtyard with a magnificent orange tree and small pool. Recommended.

GUÉLIZ AND HIVERNAGE

Bab Hotel €€€–€€€€ *corner of boulevard Mansour Eddhabi and rue Mohammed el Beqal, tel: 0524-43 52 50, www.babhotelmarrakech. com.* For those who would rather avoid the medina, the Bab Hotel is an urban sanctuary and temple to modernism and minimalism. There is no exoticism here – just fresh white rooms, slate-floored bathrooms and a hip bar and restaurant downstairs that is always lively.

Suite Hotel €€–€€€ *Rue Harroun Errachid, tel: 0524-42 45 40, www.suitehotel.com.* The Suite Hotel is excellent value for money. Each of the 112 rooms (including reduced mobility rooms) offers a living space with TV and small kitchen. There is a bar where you can buy freshly prepared dishes to eat in your room, a pool, fitness centre, broadband and the use of a car for stays of four nights or more.

Hotel Toulousain € *44 rue Tariq ibn Ziad, tel: 0524-43 00 33, www. hoteltoulousain.com.* This long-established budget hotel, where beat writer William Burroughs and his friends used to hang out, is still going strong with basic but clean rooms in the heart of the new town.

PALMERAIE

Dar Zemora €€€–€€€€ *Rue el Aandalib, Palmeraie, tel: 0524-32 82 00, www.darzemora.com.* This country-style retreat set in spacious grounds is a wonderful place to get away from it all. With a pavilion to laze about in, a delicious pool and rose-filled gardens that flicker with hundreds of candles at night, Dar Zemora is also intimate: there are just three bedrooms and three suites, all with private terraces.

Les Deux Tours €€–€€€ *Douar Abiad, tel: 0524-32 95 25, www. les-deux-tours.com.* Les Deux Tours is one of the oldest hotels in the Palmeraie. Built by Tunisian architect, Charles Boccara, it still feels like the private home it once was. The gardens are lush, the pool sublime and all the rooms are unique – some even have private plunge pools. Understated and affordable luxury in a romantic setting.

Jnane Tamsna €€€€€ *Douar Abiad, tel: 0524-32 84 84, www.jnane. com.* These five beautiful villas are set in a splendid perfumed garden. Each villa has its own pool, and the rooms are the latest in African-Middle Eastern chic. Cooking classes, yoga, reflexology, massage and gardening lessons for kids are all on offer.

OURIKA AND HIGH ATLAS

Kasbah Bab Ourika €€€–€€€€ *Ourika Valley, tel: 0668-74 95 47, www.kasbahbabourika.com.* This hotel is majestically perched on a hilltop in the lush Ourika Valley with 360-degree panoramic views over traditional Berber villages, the Atlas Mountains and the lush river valley below. It offers beautiful rooms and the chance to relax in the gardens where there's a pool, or to trek in the gorgeous surroundings.

Kasbah du Toubkal €€–€€€€€ *Imlil, Asni (60km/38 miles from Marrakech), tel: 0524-48 56 11, www.kasbahdutoubkal.com.* The Kasbah du Toubkal, situated at the foot of Jbel Toubkal, the highest peak in North Africa, is an extraordinary hotel run by a Brit together with local Berbers. The home of a local ruler was transformed into a range of accommodation from a comfortable mountain refuge to luxury suites with incredible views. The Kasbah is so much more than a hotel: it is a place of meditation for those seeking total peace and quiet. The hotel runs a lodge further into the mountains so you can walk between the two.

CASCADES D'OUZOUD

Riad Cascades d'Ouzoud €€€–€€€ *Ouzoud, tel: 0662-14 38 02, www.ouzoud.com.* Perched on top of the waterfalls, this friendly and very welcoming guesthouse has nine bedrooms decorated in rustic chic with local textiles and furnishings. The owners also run treks in the surrounding countryside, and breakfast on the roof terrace is truly spectacular.

ESSAOUIRA

Hotel Beau Rivage € *145 place Moulay Hassan, tel: 0524-47 59 25, www.essaouiranet.com/beaurivage.* A recently refurbished, long-established budget hotel with views over the most popular square in town. Clean rooms with spotless private bathrooms, and a great rooftop terrace that overlooks the port and town.

Dar Loulema €€€ *2 rue Souss, tel: 0524-47 53 46, www.riadloulema. net.* All is light and calm in this stunning 18th-century *riad*, brilliantly located just off the ramparts. The rooms are all named after places in Morocco and decorated accordingly. Fantastic food on request and a beautiful roof terrace overlooking the sea.

Madada €€€ *5 rue Youssef el-Fassi, tel: 0524-47 55 12, www.madada. com.* Small guesthouse with just six very stylish and comfortable rooms, some around the roof terrace with sweeping views over the beach, the harbour and the Bay of Essaouira.

INDEX

Berlitz

Marra

Second Editi

Written by Syl
Updated by Tat
Commissioning
Copy-editor: F
Series Editor:
Production: Ty
and Rebeka Ella

No part of thi
stored in a ret
in any form o
mechanical, p
or otherwise,
permission fro
text quotation
exempted for

All Rights Re
© 2012 Apa P

Printed in Ch

Berlitz Trade
and other cou
Used under li
Investment C